Compass and a Map

A Guide for the International Business Development Manager

Mark Lamb

Published by

Forward Thinking Publishing

London, England

First published 2022

Published by Forward Thinking Publishing

Text © Mark Lamb 2022

A catalog record for this book is available from the British Library.

ISBN: 978-1-7397230-1-9

Published by Forward Thinking Publishing

Contents

Introduction 1

PART 1 - The Career Path, Mentorships and
Networks 11

CHAPTER 1 - The Career Path and Performance
Expectations 12
    Primary Job Functions 14
    Key Performance Indicators 16
    Personal Credentials 17

CHAPTER 2 - Contact Databases, External Networks
and Mentorships 19
Face-to-Face Contact 20
Contact Data Files 21
Business Card Database 22
LinkedIn 23
Networks and Networking 24
    Networking Skills Developed through Mentorship
    Relationships 25
    Networking Skills for Receptions and Conferences ... 26
    Name Recognition Networking Skill 28
    Your Network Is Only as Strong as Your Professional
    and Personal Reputation 29
    Real Networks Versus Customer Relationship
    Management Systems (CRMs) 31
    Virtual Networking Considerations 32
    Other Networking Considerations 34
The Value of Client – Supplier Trust 36
Agency Relationships Must Not Replace Direct
Relationships 36

Business Development In-Person Representation and
Key Account Management.. 37

**CHAPTER 3 - Intracompany Team Communications,
Internal Networks and Difficult Colleagues**................. 39
Internal Networks.. 39
Virtual Team Meetings... 40
Virtual Team Document Sharing....................................... 41
Considerations for Commercial Team Written
Communications... 42
Job Security, Flexibility and Multi-Division Support..... 43
Problematic Colleagues... 46

**PART 2 - International Business Development
Campaign Management, Planning and Execution**....... 49

CHAPTER 4 - The Complex Trip.................................... 50
Complex Meeting Itineraries versus Single Project
Related Meetings.. 51
Detail Illustration of a Complex Trip.............................. 51
Goals of the Trip.. 54
Network Challenges - South America Complex Trip
Illustration.. 55

CHAPTER 5 - The Travel Team..................................... 56
Travel Team Management and Leadership...................... 56
Management Approvals.. 57
Benefits of Early Management Approvals – South
American Complex Trip Illustration................................ 58
Planning Administrative Support...................................... 59
Professional 24/7 Travel Agents....................................... 59

**CHAPTER 6 - Planning Challenges and
Considerations**... 61
Visa Application and Issuance Delays.............................. 61
Time Zone Challenges.. 63
Virtual Meeting Planning – Electronic Calendar
Invitation Advantages.. 64

Meeting Scheduling Advantages of Early Planning 65
Planning Challenges- South America Complex Trip
Illustration 66
Host Country Customs and Considerations for
Planning 67
Meeting Time Control and Logistics 68
Importance of Separate Airline Ticket Booking
Records 70
Meeting Attendance Insurance 70
Planning Relative to a Commitment to an
International Career 70
Home Departure Checklist and Managing Other
Non-Business Matters 72

CHAPTER 7 - Itinerary Construction 74
Itinerary and Travel Plan Preparation 74
Significance of Pro-forma Planning 75
Template of Pro-forma Itinerary 77
Pro-forma Itinerary Construction - South America
Complex Trip Illustration 78
Optimum Trip Length 78
Importance of Early Flight Planning and
Confirmation 79
Early Flight Planning Challenge – South American
Complex Trip Illustration 79
Pro-forma Itinerary Updates 81

CHAPTER 8 - Client Communications and Other Trip
Planning Considerations 83
Meeting Agendas 83
Well-Written Client Meeting Request
Communications 85
Planning Correspondence Control 86
Meeting Reconfirmation 87
Guidelines and Considerations for Client Introductory
Communications 87

CHAPTER 9 - Client Meetings 91
Basic Principles for Conducting All First Client
Meetings – In-Person and Virtual 92
Presentation Equipment.. 95
Backup Presentation Capability 97
Pre-Meeting Client Attendee Interactions.................... 97
Meeting Agenda 98
Presentation Content 98
Presentation Delivery.. 103
Reading and Interacting with the Audience............... 103
Minutes of Meetings 104
Trip Report.. 104
Client Follow-Up 105
The Missing Presentation... 106

**CHAPTER 10 - Team Etiquette and Unique Meeting
Options** 108
Meeting Attire.. 108
Mobile Phone Etiquette.. 110
No Side Discussions... 111
Listen... 112
Data Transmission Courtesies to Clients.................... 112
Lunch and Learn Meetings... 113
The Breakfast Meeting Option for Busy Execs 114
The 'Elevator Pitch' Presentation................................ 114
Always Carry Your Tool Bag 116

**CHAPTER 11 - Cultural and Geopolitical
Considerations – Explorer Personal Skills** 117
Personal Library Tool.. 117
Cultural Adjustment Period.. 118
Cultural Comparisons.. 120
Nationality Labels 121
Cultural Immersion 122
Conform to Cultural Mannerisms 123
Political Questions... 123
Loose Lips Sink Ships 124
Sharing Culture at the Dinner Table 125

Language 126
Host Country History 128
Cultural Connectors 129
Multiple Trip Requirement for Relationship
Development 129
Host Country Key Information 130
Importance of Simple Cultural Experiences 130
Taking a Local Approach 131
No Politics or Jokes 132
Conform 133
Where are you from? 133
Cultural Training 134
Corruption 135

**PART 3 - Project Tender Responsibilities and
Future Challenges** 136

**CHAPTER 12 - The Business Development Manager's
Responsibilities for the Tender Process and Contract
Handover** 137
The Tender (Bidding) Process 138
Tender Team and Focus 139
Components of the Tender Process 139
Corporate Structures for Managing the Tender
Process 145
The Business Development Manager's
Responsibilities for the Tender 145
Ad-Hoc Tender Preparation Guidelines 148
Summary 149

**CHAPTER 13 - Post-Pandemic Inspired Challenges,
Organization and Opportunities** 151
Accelerated Change 152
Virtual Travel is Cost-Effective 153
How Will the Pandemic Affect International Business
Travel? 154
Virtual Meeting Execution 157

PART 4 - International Business Travel...................... 161

**CHAPTER 14 - In-Transit Challenges and
Hurdles – Land and Air** **162**
Basic Rules for Flight Connections 163
A Serious Need for Ground Support............................ 165
Flight Layover Lodging 167
Airline Executive Lounges... 167
Early Flight Boarding.. 168
In-Flight Use of Laptop Computers 168
En-Route Alcohol Consumption 169
Customs Rules and Regulations.................................... 170
Immigration Passport Entry Stamp on Arrival 171
Security Delays Resulting from Multiple Visas............ 172
Passport Control 173
Intra-Country Small Airline Flight Safety 173
Different Arrival and Departure Airports.................... 174
Travel Expense Control and Business Class................. 174
Auto Door Slamming.. 178
In-Transit Courtesies Therapy 178
In-Transit Restrooms 179

**CHAPTER 15 - In-Country Logistics and Hotel and
Restaurant Tools**.. **180**
Investment in Local Business Community Preferred
Hotels and Restaurants 181
Client Executive Assistant Support.............................. 182
Hotel Concierge 182
Other Hotel Considerations... 184
Restaurant 101 185
Restaurant Meeting Etiquette.. 187
Intracity Logistics 189
Avoid Rental Cars... 190
Client Company Provided Vehicle and Driver 191
Briefcase Security in Client Offices 191

CHAPTER 16 - Health, Safety and Security **193**
Viruses.. 193

Travel Medicine Resources..194
Internal Security Risk Meter..194
Airport Reception Security...195
Eating and Drinking on the Streets 196
High Profile Escorts and Security 196
Taxi Security...197
Kidnapping and Ransom Insurance Coverage 197
Intestinal Issues...200
Jet Lag...201
Flight Claustrophobia 201
Traffic Safety 202
Throw-Down Wallet 202
Personal Demeanor and Security 203
Blood Clot Risk of Long Flights...................................203
Personal Hygiene on Flights and When Executing
the Business Itinerary..204
Travel Diet...204
Security - Walking in Unsecure Areas.........................205
Pickpockets and Luggage Security 206
Health and Emergency Medivac Insurance..................207
Bed Bugs...208

**CHAPTER 17 - Control and Maintenance of Nine
Critical Travel Tools...209**
Nine Critical Tools...209
Passport...210
Security Documents..212
Second Passport 213
Financial Tools 214
    Credit Cards...214
    Cash (Emergency Reserve)......................................216
    Currency Exchange 217
    Currency Restrictions 218
    Airport Departure Taxes 219
    Online Money Transfer Platforms...........................219
    Other Cash Considerations......................................220
Safe Keeping Tools...220
Travel Team Expense Sharing 222

Mobile Phones.. 223
Computer Backup and Security................................... 225
Prescriptions and Medical Devices............................ 225
Carryon Clothing for Arrival Meetings 226
Travel Thumb Drive Back-Up for Critical Documents 226
Critical Tools and Hotel Room Service Considerations
.... 228

CHAPTER 18 - Select Travel Equipment, Tools and General International Travel Advice 229
Luggage Preferences... 229
Luggage Security.. 232
Luggage Options.. 233
Bags Always Ready and On Standby........................... 234
Small Carry-on Toiletry Bag 235
Duffel Bags.. 235
Microfiber Underwear 236
Emergency Urine Bags and Toilet Tissue.................... 236
Business Cards.. 236
Prepaid Express Mail Envelopes 237
Small Lightweight Day Pack 237
Safekeeping Products 237
Flashlights... 238
International Phone Plans... 238

CHAPTER 19 - Conclusion.. 239

PART 5 - The Toolbox.. 241
Toolbox Contents 242
Tool No. 1 – Pro-forma Trip Plan and Itinerary (Format) 243
Tool No. 2 – Checklist - International Business Trip Planning – (Example) 246
Tool No. 3 – Client Meeting Request – (Example) 250
Tool No. 4 – Agenda - Client In-Person Meeting (Format) 251
Tool No. 5 – Agenda – Virtual Client Meeting (Format) 253

Tool No. 6 – Checklist - Home Departure (Example) 255
Tool No. 7 – Checklist - Comprehensive Travel Packing – Business and Personal (Example) 257

Suggested Further Reading 261

About the Author 262

*To my encouraging and patient wife Patricia, and the
support and knowledge of friends
John Hartono, Allan Ross, Douglas Miller,
Michael Young, Barbara Smith, Rebecca McElroy
and Pieter Bakker.*

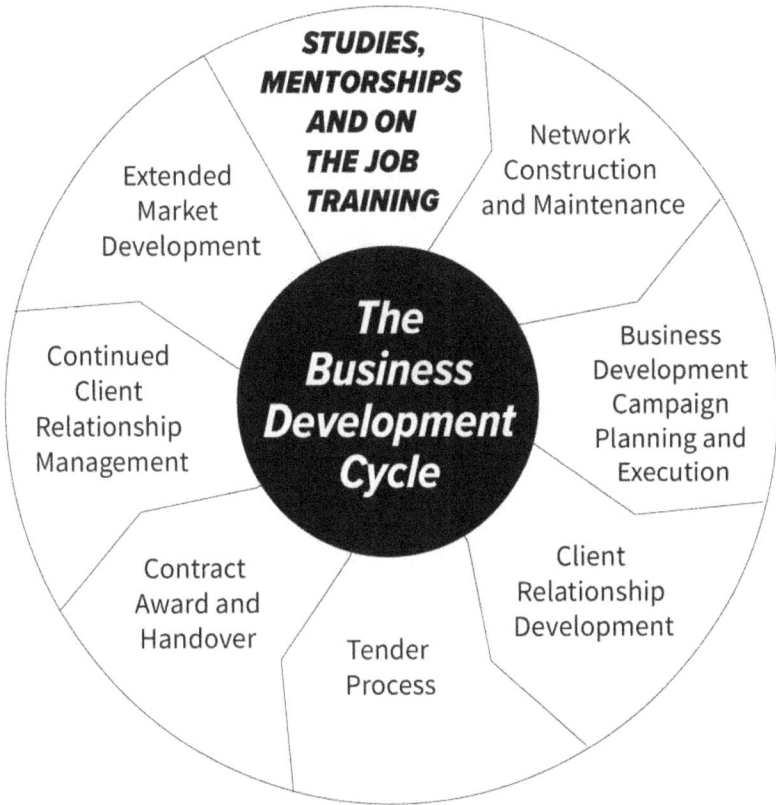

STUDIES, MENTORSHIPS AND ON THE JOB TRAINING

Network Construction and Maintenance

The Business Development Cycle

Business Development Campaign Planning and Execution

Client Relationship Development

Tender Process

Contract Award and Handover

Continued Client Relationship Management

Extended Market Development

Introduction

IN QUASI-RETIREMENT, I HAVE sought to write this book to share my career experience with the goal of enhancing your success in developing international markets and the award of profitable contracts. The experience I share will shorten your learning curve in each phase of the business development cycle: network development, business trip planning and execution, the tender process, through the handover of awarded contracts to operations groups. The travel guidance I provide will be helpful to all who travel globally.

You may have recently assumed international business development responsibilities or you are a seasoned professional. The book you are about to read presents information I needed but did not have when I began my international business career and have relied on since. I share over 45 years of experience with you, of which the last 25 were committed to international business development activities. My career began with Ernst and Young as a Certified Public Accountant (CPA). The skillsets developed in public accounting have been instrumental to my career in international business development, principally organization, planning, financial analysis, writing, and supervision and development of younger colleagues.

For me, international business travel has always been an adventure, challenging and most importantly, fun. I look forward to each business trip as a learning experience. I take every opportunity to travel and my passports reflect this with visa stamps from at least 75 of the world's 195 countries, representing well over 2 million air miles traveled. I took the time to record useful information and experiences in journals documenting travel mistakes, ideas, culture and cuisine. These journal entries and a career of international and domestic business experience are the basis of this book.

As a professional in this field, your international travel will be heavy. You will have complete responsibility for planning and managing 'complex' global business development campaigns. To be successful, you must first know your service or product operationally and technically well, preferably further supported by hands-on experience. Secondly, you must develop superior networking, organization, planning and presentation skills. Ideally, you develop these abilities over time as a business development team member or through formal mentorship programs designed to transfer knowledge from experienced, typically older colleagues, to younger colleagues.

We all learn from our mistakes. I did not have the benefits of a formal mentorship program for my first complex international business trip. I now clearly understand what Oscar Wilde meant when he said, "Experience is the name we give our mistakes." Throughout the book, I provide guidance and share actual experiences you can use to shorten your learning curve. I want you to be instrumental in leading business development campaigns that result in profitable contract awards for your company and your professional advancement. The information that I share in this book will be vital to your long-term success.

During periods of economic downturn, companies typically first reduce employment costs. Those affected are usually the older,

higher-paid and more experienced employees. Companies that have not implemented effective mentoring or coaching programs lose the opportunity for valuable knowledge transfer to younger colleagues. The knowledge and experience are often lost forever. A primary goal of this book is to encourage filling this information transfer gap.

Life-changing random events, such as wars, pandemics, financial meltdowns and yet-to-be-named calamities will occur unexpectedly. An insightful professional will adjust quickly, adapt, take advantage of the situation, and focus on the established business goals. Throughout the book, I emphasize that the basic principles of networking, planning and executing business development plans remain the same after a mega-event as before the event. We must continuously modify the processes for achieving the goals to offset any unforeseen obstacles. For example, during the COVID-19 pandemic, international travel was reduced or temporarily halted and we were forced to depend on virtual communications with our clients, colleagues, partners and suppliers. Extraordinary business planning, travel, and execution techniques are required for all business climates but are most significant during and following mega-events such as the COVID-19 pandemic.

Chapter 4 presents a recent business development campaign to Guyana, Suriname, Trinidad and Colombia. This trip is what I refer to throughout the book as a 'complex trip', having the following characteristics:

1. Multiple countries and cities visited, often new to you and your company.
2. Numerous back-to-back market and client development meetings.
3. A week or more of meetings and travel.

For this trip, I present the business goals and summarize the time records I maintained for planning and executing this complex trip to

an area of the world where our company was not previously known and our network of contacts was limited. The trip covered 4 countries and included 35 meetings in 15 days - requiring at least 60 hours of planning over 2.5 months. Further challenging the trip was a two-week travel limitation set by our management. Actual international travel experiences, such as this, are presented to guide you through planning similar market development campaigns. If you do not arrive in the targeted countries, the business goals will not be realized.

This work has brought to my attention the versatility and multi-skillset capabilities of the successful international business development professional. The successful person will be adventurous, well-rounded, technically savvy, personable and culturally adaptable. I discuss these and many preferred qualities for the profession in Chapter 1.

The book presents more than 300 takeaways to guide you in the business development process. The points made are based on my personal experiences and are offered as guidance only. Everyone will conduct their work using varying approaches and methods influenced by culture, industry, age group or generation and many other factors. The points I emphasize have worked for me and should be adjusted to fit the circumstances. With this book in your toolbox, consider it as a compass and a map that will be instrumental in guiding you through a career in international business.

How to use this book?

I have broken the book down into five parts:

- Part 1 – The Career Path, External and Internal Networks;
- Part 2 – International Business Development Campaign Management, Planning and Execution;
- Part 3 – Project Tender Responsibilities and Future Challenges;

- Part 4 – International Business Travel; and
- Part 5 – The Toolbox.

Below I briefly summarized the topics in each part. My advice would be first to scan the chapters, then to use the book as you would for a manual or guide.

Chapter 1 – The Career Path and Performance Expectations

This chapter discusses the Key Performance Indicators and the skillsets that the successful international business development manager will employ throughout the business development cycle, emphasizing the importance of broad-based prior experience.

Chapter 2 – Contact Databases, External Network Development Skills and Mentorships

Success in a business development career is dependent on your ability to build, protect and maintain productive external and internal networks. I review in-person and virtual networking skills and present several stories and examples to illustrate the social networking skills of extraordinarily successful business development professionals and executives. I also discuss formal and informal mentorship programs designed to shorten your learning curve, emphasizing that your responsibility is to find a mentor if your company does not have a formal mentorship program.

Chapter 3 – Intracompany Communications, Internal Networks and Difficult Colleagues

Developing networks within your company is equally important as external client relationship development. This chapter explains how collaborating closely with international colleagues, possibly in unrelated product divisions, can be a powerful tool to identify and develop business opportunities. I emphasize the importance of

returning value to your internal networks for information and support received. Vital to your career is managing internal issues with other colleagues and difficult situations you will invariably encounter as you negotiate your winding career path.

Chapter 4 – The 'Complex' Trip

International market development campaigns often demand a complex itinerary and travel plan, requiring many client meetings in multiple cities and countries within a limited time. Planning and executing successful complex business development trips requires extensive planning and organization. This chapter presents an actual four-country business development trip illustrating the business development manager's responsibilities for planning and managing a complex international business development campaign.

Chapter 5 – The Travel Team

This chapter reviews the business development manager's leadership role in managing the business development campaign and directing a team of colleagues, administrative support, travel agents and coordinating travel planning with upper-level managers.

Chapter 6 – Planning Challenges and Considerations

International travel planning and execution are full of challenges that are not present in domestic travel. If not effectively managed, the challenges can easily cause the failure of achieving the business goals. This chapter highlights the common planning challenges faced and presents options for managing them.

Chapter 7 – Itinerary Construction

A complex international business development trip's success is highly dependent on a strategically organized, well-planned itinerary. The

travel plan and meeting order must support the business goals. This chapter discusses optimum trip time, advantages of early planning, pro-forma itinerary preparation techniques, and personal travel examples.

Chapter 8 – Client Communications and Other Trip Planning Considerations

This chapter reviews the value of well-written and concise client communications. It is necessary to grab the client's attention to schedule the all-important first introductory meeting. This chapter provides detailed guidelines for client communications. I also discuss the requirement to stay abroad for the time required to execute a heavy itinerary in a single trip, emphasizing the traveling challenges of a post-pandemic era.

Chapter 9 – Client Meetings

You will typically have about one hour to present your company's capabilities for the project and convince the client that your company can deliver those requirements. This chapter will guide you through the meeting planning and execution process, emphasizing that your 'presentation' is not the PowerPoint.

Chapter 10 – Team Etiquette and Unique Meeting Options

The client's first impression of your company must be a high potential long-term partner who can support and complement their project needs. A wrong impression may close the project opportunity. This chapter guides in developing client relationships when working with other cultures.

Chapter 11 - Cultural and Geopolitical Considerations- Explorer Personal Skills

To work successfully in global markets, we must be accepted by a multi-cultural client base and communicate a sincere interest in their cultures. I review the importance of sharing culture at the dinner table, knowledge of the local language and host country history.

Chapter 12 – The Business Development Manager's Responsibilities for the Tender Process and Contract Handover

The end goal of the business development cycle is the award of profitable contracts and the establishment of long-term client relationships. This chapter discusses your responsibilities for the tender (or bidding) process, which will vary based on your company's size and if your company has a dedicated tendering department. I emphasize that the business development manager must continue as the client's primary interface and point person in all tender organization structures.

Chapter 13 – Post-Pandemic Inspired Challenges, Organization and Opportunities

The basic principles of networking, planning and executing business development activities during and post-pandemic do not change. The primary shift is reduced travel and limited face-to-face client and colleague contact. This chapter emphasizes virtual meeting planning and the proper use of digital communication tools and related new technology.

Chapter 14 - In-Transit Challenges and Hurdles – Land and Air

If you do not arrive at your destination, you will not accomplish the business goals. In this chapter, I share personal stories and experiences, emphasizing travel mistakes we all make because we

depend on preconceived notions, impressions, and personal biases. The pressures of a complex international business development campaign often challenge our common sense and we must be fully aware of those challenges.

Chapter 15 - In-Country Logistics, Hotel and Restaurant Tools

Once in the country, we must rely on and effectively utilize local resources such as hotel services, restaurants, transportation services and more. This chapter highlights the importance of selecting high-quality and well-located hotels and restaurants that meet the client's expectations and have the resources necessary to support the business development effort. In this chapter, I discuss restaurant etiquette, intra-meeting logistics and the value of support from the client's executive assistant, the hotel concierge and much more.

Chapter 16 - Health, Safety and Security

Global business travelers are constantly exposed to health, safety and security risks that must be identified and mitigated to the extent possible. The chapter provides advice and guidance based on firsthand experiences, such as security issues, intestinal problems and other threats confronting the international business traveler.

Chapter 17 - Control and Maintenance of Nine Critical Travel Tools

At least nine travel tools are critical to an international business development trip and they must be protected. The loss of one or more of these tools can terminate the trip, and not having certain tools will test the most experienced professional.

Chapter 18 - Select Travel Equipment and Tools

As I traveled worldwide, I maintained journals and made notes of travel tools and equipment that worked well. I also made notes of any

tools I needed but had no access to on those trips. This chapter provides guidance for both business and leisure travelers.

The Toolbox

The Toolbox presents document formats and checklists I have found helpful to my travels and assist in maintaining focus on the business. All checklists should be modified to meet your specific needs.

In closing this Introduction, I am confident that you will find the tools and information presented in the following chapters invaluable as you negotiate an international business development or commercial career, potentially leading to executive positions that demand internationally savvy candidates who bring wide-based generalist capabilities and who are multi-culturally adaptable. For the graduating student, I am sure that the knowledge shared will effectively elevate interview confidence and performance, arming you with the knowledge that may make the interviewer perceive you as having prior international business experience. Chapter 1 begins by reviewing the multiple career paths to international business development positions, job functions and responsibilities, and Key Performance Indicators for success.

Part 1
The Career Path, Mentorships and Networks

CHAPTER 1

The Career Path and
Performance
Expectations

THIS CHAPTER OUTLINES THE performance expectations for international business development professionals, highlights the importance of accumulated career experience, and emphasizes that a career path will be full of surprising bends and turns.

We live in an age of rapid digitalization, globalization and innovation. The rate of change is swift and stressful, making career planning challenging. Unlike previous generations, you will most likely work for multiple companies over your career, possibly in different professions. Unplanned and unforeseeable events will cause you to recalibrate direction and remap your career path, as was my experience.

I always wanted to work internationally and travel globally in a position where I could best maximize the value of my strengths. Not until the last half of my career were opportunities presented that fit precisely within my long-term professional plan. Persevering, one will find a career position that effectively synchronizes strengths and experience to achieve a high level of job satisfaction. All the experience accumulated along the way is beneficial to an international business development career. As a global business development manager, you will rely on a toolbox full of multi-capability experiences to satisfy the performance expectations discussed below. As I explain in the following stories, my career direction unexpectedly changed multiple times, and these events were instrumental in steering me to an exciting 25-year career in international business development.

Economic circumstances can quickly alter one's career direction, as the mid-1980's downturn in the petroleum industry did to mine. My company's business virtually came to a standstill in a matter of weeks. I was the company's Chief Financial Officer (CFO). The owner walked into my office and said, "Business is terrible. We don't need accountants. We need people who can increase sales and develop new business opportunities. Can you do that?" That was the exact moment that I put my CPA certificate in my desk drawer, realigned my career direction to meet the need (and market demand) and focused on sales and developing new business opportunities; however, I continued to rely on my previous financial experience. The sales team happily gifted me the customer accounts they liked the least. These were my best customers because they were my first customers – none to compare them to. I did not know the difference between the easier to deal with customers (which the other salespeople retained) and the more challenging clients. From that point forward, I welcomed difficult client accounts for the challenges they presented.

Two more examples of events that significantly changed my career's direction were the Exxon Valdez oil spill and, interestingly, a

West Texas rattlesnake. The super oil tanker, Exxon Valdez, grounded on a rock in Prince William Sound off the Alaskan coast and spilled over 11 million US gallons of crude oil into the pristine waters. This single event effectively ushered in a whole new era of professionalism in the oil and gas industry and set new standards for quality of operations. The Good Old Boy approach to business development and marketing, which predominated my industry, was no longer acceptable to many clients, especially the larger corporations. A whole new level of professionalism was required from business development and marketing professionals.

A West Texas rattlesnake had also redirected my career path. As a young CPA at Ernst and Young, my boss called me into his office on a Friday and told me that I would receive a call from our client on Monday, who would offer me the position of CFO. I felt confident that the offer would be an excellent career change opportunity. Monday morning, my boss called me back into his office to tell me that the client, who was to offer me the position that day, had died over the weekend from a rattlesnake bite while hunting quail in West Texas. Unexpectedly, a giant rattlesnake had abruptly changed my professional plan. You have no control over events that can and will change your career's direction.

Considering the above, let us look at expectations and skillsets for the position.

Primary Job Functions

Most international business development job position requirements and responsibilities will typically include the following functions:

1.   Global market analysis, reporting and presentation.
2.   Geographic specific market analysis, reporting and presentation.

3. Competition identification and Strengths, Weaknesses, Opportunities and Threats (SWOT) analysis, reporting and presentation.
4. Network construction, development and maintenance.
5. Marketing plan development.
6. Client database system management.
7. Project identification and targeted client development plan.
8. Market development trip planning and execution.
9. Tender (or bid) process procurement and qualification (Requests for Proposals (RFPs)).
10. Tender (or bid) management and preparation, including client interface during the tender process.
11. Contract review and analysis.
12. Awarded project handover to operations teams or project managers.
13. Continued client relationship management.

As the list indicates, the responsibilities require differing degrees of expertise in finance, business law, contracting, personnel management, project management, network development, writing skills and much more. As a result, the career is well represented by professionals with prior experience from a wide range of fields. Few careers require professionals who can effectively manage such a wide range of responsibilities.

In his book *Range: Why Generalist Triumph in a Specialized World*, David Epstein states, "what the world needs now are generalists with a wide array of experiences and perspectives." The world needs 'people with range'. He says that in the long run, people who 'leapfrog' around will eventually land on something that is a perfect fit, in which they can leverage that breadth of experience, skill and knowledge they gained in the process which leads to a more fulfilling life as well. He goes on to say that systems that demand hyper-specialization "would have you decide what you should be before figuring out who you are." Epstein also discusses the inability of some specialists to think

creatively. Clearly, today's business development professional must develop generalist skill sets and be capable of functioning in a comprehensive range of responsibilities.

Key Performance Indicators

Hiring the wrong person for managerial and executive positions is costly for both employees and the company. A Wall Street Journal article (January 7, 2022) states, "Staff turnover is pricey—it costs an estimated one-half to two times an employee's annual salary to replace her. Plus, it's disruptive to client relationships and the morale of staffers left behind." Valuable time is lost in the client development process and the time to refill the position can be excessive. Evaluating candidates based upon well-written, continuously updated and focused Key Performance Indicators (KPIs), combined with aptitude and personality tests, best ensure the selection and retention of qualified candidates for international business positions.

KPIs for international business development positions will vary between companies, industries and geographic regions. The following list is representative:

<u>Personal</u>

1. Personal Presentation
2. Self-Confidence
3. Sense of Humor
4. Team Player
5. Intercultural Skills, Relationships, Positive Mannerisms, Empathy and Sensitivity
6. Adventurous Attitude
7. Team Leadership and Intra-Team Problem Resolution Capabilities

Cultural

1. Strong Cultural Interests
2. Desire to Travel
3. Vision
4. Foreign Language Skills

Development Skills

1. Networking Skills
2. Out of the Box Thinker
3. Mentorship
4. Big Picture Ability

Technical and Administrative

1. Organizational Skills
2. Writing Skills
3. Technical Knowledge
4. Presentation Preparation and Delivery

Study performance expectations at the front end of the job – not after your first performance review. You must be clear about management's expectations from your performance and focus all networking, planning, and execution activities on accomplishing those expectations.

Personal Credentials

The human resources process for evaluating candidates for international positions must identify their underlying interests in the career. The preferred candidate may live in a world thoroughly influenced by multiculturalism and geopolitical interests. For example, their office and home may be full of books, photos and memorabilia from the countries they have or plan to travel to. They may follow international news on BBC or other international sources.

Many will own a lovely globe and might have a world map on the wall pinned with places traveled. They will have established international relationships and maintain regular contact with the networks developed through these travels. Also, their vacations further exemplify their global interests, typically traveling to parts of the world they had previously visited on business trips—many times to places that other people would not consider for a vacation. The interview process must identify these areas of the candidate's interest.

Now that we have discussed the requirements and skillsets for the position let us jump into the book's meat: networking, international business development campaign planning, execution and international business travel.

CHAPTER 2

Contact Databases, External Networks and Mentorships

A POWERFUL BUSINESS NETWORK is the most valuable resource in your toolbox. Protect it, maintain it, and continuously expand it. These connections are the foundation of your career. In this chapter, I emphasize that your success depends on an effective network and provide guidance on building, maintaining, and protecting this asset.

If you are a college student, your network is relatively small and limited to fellow students, professors, friends, and family. Your network as a young employee is also comparatively small. Now is the time to focus on developing and honing the networking skills you will depend on for an entire career. Below I discuss time-proven methods and examples you can use to grow, maintain and protect your network.

Face-to-Face Contact

Relationship development is highly dependent on person-to-person contact. For example, during the peaks of the COVID-19 pandemic, interpersonal interactions were reliant on virtual technologies. We quickly realized how vital person-to-person communications are to building external client networks and internal networks with colleagues. At the same time, we learned that most office-based employees can work efficiently from home offices, eliminating commuting time and transportation costs.

How have impersonal digital communications affected our ability to network and build effective relationships? An article in the Wall Street Journal, entitled 'The Science of Staying Connected', reviewed the effects of high-tech communications on business relationships noting that "social interaction is a biological requirement" and that "genuine psychological contact depends on infinitesimal cues that the human brain picks up when someone is talking directly to us." This science emphasizes that technology will reduce face-to face-communications but cannot replace direct person-to-person contact to build networks and client relationships.

I recently supported a Latin American client with a bid proposal. Our tender team of five was based in four countries. The COVID-19 pandemic forced our team to work remotely from our home offices. Working remotely presented many challenges, including working from multiple time zones; one team member was based in Lithuania, eight hours ahead of Houston, and one team member was three hours earlier. Having never met the team and after working remotely for over three months, including 15 team video conferences, I felt that I knew each team member quite well. One week before the proposal's due date, we recognized that we must sit together in person to finish the work, so I traveled to Mexico City and worked shoulder-to-shoulder with the tender team manager to complete the proposal. After one day of working face-to-face and interacting in person, I first

fully appreciated my colleague's skills and capabilities. The virtual meeting technology we first depended on to complete this project was incapable of effectively transmitting the discussions and interactions necessary to deliver a quality proposal. The week working together in Mexico City was incredibly productive and efficient. This experience, while writing this book, clearly demonstrated to me the incredible importance of face-to-face contact. Virtual communications will not effectively replace person-to-person interactions.

Contact Data Files

You probably document your network in applications such as Microsoft Outlook. Unfortunately, computers crash or are stolen, and we do not have complete control of cloud data storage. If you unexpectedly lose your job, you typically immediately surrender your company-owned laptop computer, mobile phone and stored contact files. I am aware of situations where senior managers with large corporations, during severe economic downturns, were unexpectedly laid off from their jobs. Their company computers and phones were seized, and the company would not give them a copy of their contact database or any other information stored on the company-owned equipment. As a result, they never fully recovered the many connections they brought to the company from previous employments. I had a similar experience and asked my former employer for a copy of my contacts to learn that IT had erased the hard disk. Fortunately, I had made a reasonably current backup on a portable hard drive. Contact data files represent a career accumulation of business and personal contacts and must be routinely backed up on at least one, preferably two, portable external hard drives, then securely stored. Back up any other important files on your company-owned devices and set up a monthly backup reminder on your calendar.

A poorly maintained network quickly becomes cold, old and stale and will go missing in an amazingly brief period. Today, people are highly mobile and frequently change employers. Maintaining frequent communication with your network electronically and through routine face-to-face visits is essential. If there is no immediate business reason to connect, consider sharing an industry-related article, technical paper, or other information, adding a short, personalized transmittal note. You should never send a mass mailing of information to your contacts for relationship maintenance purposes. Network maintenance communications should be personally written on a one-on-one basis. For those situations where you must mass mail data to numerous contacts, never reveal the client addresses on the face of an email - always send with addressees in blind copy (BCC). Clients and others who have entrusted you with their contact information expect you to keep it confidential.

An excellent method for rapidly growing your network and contact database is for each email received, immediately add the sender and those copied to your contact database. People copied on the email are involved with the communication subject and may provide future value to your network. Emails typically have sender signature information, including the company name, website, title and phone numbers. Adding these contacts to your database takes only a few seconds and should become automatic for each email received. You should timestamp each updated contact data file following the contact's last name (i.e., John Smith (2022)). This procedure ensures that you are using the latest email address.

Business Card Database

I have accumulated thousands of business cards over my career. An excellent habit is to make appropriate notes on the back of business cards that will be helpful reminders when following up. Business cards can be conveniently filed in three-ring binders using

plastic business card filing sheets. The global traveler should file cards, first alphabetically by country. If you file all cards alphabetically by the company without regard to country, you will have to sort through and rearrange all the cards when preparing for a trip. When organizing the trip plan, you can copy the appropriate country's card sheets and attach them to the itinerary for quick reference during the trip.

Excellent business card scanning apps automatically file contact information into your contact database. When using these apps, double-check to ensure that the data copies correctly into the database. Unfortunately, these scanning apps are not 100% accurate, primarily because cards have different formats. After scanning the card, make a notation on its face, indicating that it is copied to your database.

People around the world have different customs for exchanging business cards. For example, in Asian countries, the cards are exchanged respectfully using both hands instead of the informal exchanges in many Western countries. It is considerate to have separate cards printed in the local language or print the foreign language card on the back of your home language business card. Clients will always appreciate your effort to present a card printed in the local language, especially in countries using different writing systems and alphabets.

LinkedIn

LinkedIn is a handy tool for identifying, researching and connecting with targeted companies and clients. Try to connect with the client on LinkedIn before or immediately after the first meeting. I regret not developing this habit when LinkedIn first became available. Your LinkedIn site must be well-organized, kept current, and meet your company's standards. Many clients will first review your LinkedIn account and your company's website before responding to a meeting request.

LinkedIn is an excellent cold call tool for connecting with companies you have been unsuccessful reaching through your network. However, my opinion is that LinkedIn should not be the primary platform for requesting meetings. Always exhaust direct and indirect network references before requesting a client meeting via LinkedIn.

Your client's biographical information is frequently available on LinkedIn, including professional background, university studies, prior employment, technical papers and more. This information is useful for preparing introductory emails, introducing your company and requesting introductory meetings.

LinkedIn is a powerful business development and sales tool and I highly suggest becoming thoroughly familiar with its capabilities and maximizing its value in the business development effort.

Networks and Networking

One of the most important networking points to remember is that the process requires a give-and-take approach. To develop effective itineraries and secure meetings, you will rely on others within your direct and indirect network for referrals and client contact information. You must share knowledge and information with your network of roughly equal values. Many do not consider this point sufficiently; they always ask for information but never give it. After receiving contact information from your network, immediately ask what you can do for them in return. How can you help them? Remember that network sharing is a 'two-way street' - you must support and nourish information resources if you expect their continued support and assistance.

Networking Skills Developed through Mentorship Relationships

Formal corporate mentoring programs are typically reserved for the younger and more talented employees that companies want to retain and cultivate into managers and executives. Mentoring shortens the employee's learning curve and increases productivity. A mentor-mentee approach for training business development managers is, of course, most effective when the mentor has extensive international experience and is willing to share their large contact network. Absent a formal program, the more senior colleagues often take possession of their contacts. They are often reluctant to share their client contact information, even though the company compensated them for developing the relationships. Mentorship programs should help overcome this problem.

Networking skills develop naturally over time. The opportunity to collaborate closely with a professional networker in a mentoring relationship expedites the learning process. Unfortunately, I did not have the chance to participate in formal mentorship programs, so I sought and established informal mentor relationships with those I recognized as having the skills and capabilities I wanted to develop. These individuals were not always inside my company. Still, they were recognized in my industry for having a nose for finding new business opportunities and were well known for their ability to close large contracts and acquisitions. After working with and around these professionals, it was evident that their consistent winning performance and success were attributed to their networking skills, as the following story exemplifies.

Now a close friend, this European spent much of his career living and working in South America. I first met him on a Caribbean Island where his company aggressively competed to acquire a large petroleum terminal facility on the island. This gentleman arrived on the island with a focused plan to quickly build a solid local network to

achieve his business goal of acquiring the targeted company. His networking plan was broad and included top government officials, island community business leaders, key people within the target company and other influential individuals on the island. He also made it a point to develop relationships with ordinary people. I watched this professional rapidly build an effective and winning local network in less than one month. I immediately recognized this person as a perfect mentor. Look around your organization for experienced colleagues you admire, can learn from, and respect their networking capabilities and professionalism. If you cannot find a mentor within your organization but know of one in another company, consider working for them.

Networking Skills for Receptions and Conferences

You may have attended social or industry-related receptions and you did not recognize anyone in the room? Perhaps you took something to drink or eat, then soon left the affair? Alternatively, you stayed and started working the crowd and networking. For many of us, mixing with and into a strange crowd is tough, even intimidating. Many people are terrified when interacting with a large group of people they do not know. These circumstances present opportunities to overcome this fear. Take advantage of the situation.

First, look for a person standing alone on the group's perimeter (there is always one or more) who also appears not to know any of the attendees. Introduce yourself and open a casual discussion about the conference or social gathering. Next, look around for another person similarly standing nearby; then invite them to join in the discussion. Now that you have broken the ice and feel more comfortable, excuse yourself, move around the room, identify another small group, introduce yourself and ask if you might join in the conversation. Look for facial cues and openings to start or join a conversation and avoid interrupting small groups of two or three

people who appear to be colleagues or friends. Continue the process. Working the crowd is not easy at first, but as a business development professional, you must push yourself to learn this networking skill. You will soon minimize your fear level and be amazed at the number of valuable contacts made. Any industry connection you make is one that you otherwise would have missed had you walked out of the reception soon after arriving. It is like Ernest Hemingway said, "One cat leads to another."

When attending industry conferences, make every effort to meet as many attendees as possible. Request a list of participants before the conference and prioritize those most important to your business. Then, during the conference, focus on meeting and talking to each targeted contact. If the total number of conference attendees is small, make it your goal to meet and speak with all attendees, who will notice and appreciate your networking skills and effort to meet everyone. Conference attendees who work the crowd stand out.

Another effective conference-related development tool is to host a dinner or small reception. Your event can be as simple as inviting a small group to meet at the bar at your expense. The gathering should not conflict with event programs or your employer's events but compliment them. Other options are to invite a small group to dinner the night before the conference or to breakfast during the conference.

One of my conference and reception pet peeves is to see a large group of my colleagues, for whom our company has invested in the conference, huddle together in a cluster and carry on as if they had not seen each other for years when in fact, they work together in the same office. Indeed, these colleagues were not optimizing the company's financial investment nor maximizing the opportunity to expand their business networks. Management should ascertain that employees selected to attend conferences generate the company's highest overall benefit from the investment. Make every effort to

maximize the return on the company's investment in industry conferences through active networking.

Name Recognition Networking Skill

Name recognition skills are a robust and effective business development tool. As business development professionals, we must learn techniques to memorize the names of those we meet at business and social affairs, address them by name and repeat their names and what they do as we communicate with others. Remembering and using a person's name creates a comfort level that demonstrates a stronger personal connection. Think about how you feel when people remember your name, address you accordingly, or introduce you to others by name, company affiliation and position.

I recently attended the spectacular wedding of a relative at a beautiful Utah ski resort that included 300 guests and lasted three full days. The groom's father was the retired Chairman of one of the largest financial institutions in the US. Granted, it was his responsibility to meet and greet all the guests, but his name recognition skills were extraordinary.

For three days, I watched him work the large crowd of guests, mostly friends of the wedding couple, whom I assume he had not previously met. I noticed he was continually moving, meeting, greeting and chatting with guests. Most astonishing was that he remembered everyone's name and something about each he had learned through his networking discussions. I have known others who were masters at remembering names, but this was the first time I had watched someone start from zero and go to 300 in less than three days. Also, his presence in the room was magnetic and you quickly saw that he stood out from the crowd and was a person you would like to know and could easily approach. On the last day of the event, there was a check-out guest breakfast, and he was the first to arrive and he

continued to work the crowd, greeting everyone by name and thanking them for coming to the wedding. Without a doubt, this capability is now natural to him, and he has maintained this skill sharp through practice. I am sure that he employed the same skills throughout his successful career. He would also be an excellent mentor.

During an early morning walk in Houston's Memorial Park, I saw former US Secretary of State James Baker walking ahead of me. I caught up with him, introduced myself, and we walked and talked for a short distance. I have enormous admiration for the Secretary, his incredible international diplomacy skills and his contribution to Rice University through the Baker Institute in Houston. I have signed copies of all the Secretary's books in my library, including *Work Hard, Study...and Keep Out of Politics!, Adventures and Lessons from an Unexpected Public Life* and *The Politics of Diplomacy – Revolution, War & Peace, 1989 -1992*. The Secretary said he likes to walk two miles at least three times a week, which is impressive at 91 years, especially in the Houston July heat. We shook hands and he then said, "Good to see you, Mark!" as if we were old friends. I am always impressed when someone remembers my name after such a short, or for that matter, any conversation – especially from a person the Secretary's age. His remembering my name made me feel special, particularly from such an influential person. His name recognition skill is incredible, and without a doubt, I am sure that this tool has been vital to his international diplomacy and success in building his networks.

Your Network Is Only as Strong as Your Professional and Personal Reputation

Network connections are your most valuable career resource, and your industry network is only as strong as your reputation within that industry. A single mistake can severely impair or destroy your hard-earned reputation and your network, as well as destroy a career. Unfortunately, you cannot purchase global reputation insurance, and

even Lloyds of London will not insure personal reputations. Once wrecked, your reputation and your network may not be salvageable. Only you can protect your reputation and, if damaged, only you can attempt to save and rebuild it. If you make a reputation-damaging mistake, you must take full responsibility and act immediately. With the speed of social media, reputations can be damaged or destroyed rapidly. As Mark Twain said, "A lie can travel halfway around the world while the truth is putting on its shoes." That was pre-social media.

I am closely aware of situations where colleagues and others damaged or destroyed their hard-earned reputation within their industry through improper business dealings. Suddenly, their hard-earned network became useless. In most instances, they were forced to leave the industry they had worked for an entire career and were driven to start over in a different and unrelated industry, quite often in much less lucrative careers. If you find yourself in this situation, you must quickly do everything in your power to survive.

One significant risk of reputation damage for the business development professional (as for any professional who entertains clients) is the potential consequences of driving a vehicle after a client dinner or other event and having consumed alcohol. Awareness of and respect for the associated risks are much better today than when I was young and had client development responsibilities. You should never operate a motor vehicle after drinking alcoholic beverages at these functions. I know of several situations where persons' careers were devastated after being charged with driving a vehicle while intoxicated (DWI), arrested, spending at least a night in jail, and their driver's licenses suspended for a prolonged time. Not only was their reputation damaged by the stigma of the incident, but they were unable to adequately perform their work responsibilities without the use of a motor vehicle. In a worst-case scenario, a pedestrian or cyclist is hit, injured or killed, and the resulting financial losses have the potential of wiping out your hard-earned net worth. Take a taxi or hire a car service and charge the cost on your expense report. If you are

expected to entertain clients, it is only reasonable that your employer reimburses you for these costs.

At a presentation to a master's program class at Rice University, one student asked me for two key takeaway recommendations from my career experience. Without thinking, I immediately told the class that my advice is, firstly, to protect your reputation and integrity at all costs. Secondly, is to directly focus on network-building skills, supported by tools like LinkedIn, Contacts and Outlook. Today, if asked again, I would still make the same two recommendations to the students. Build your reputation based on honesty and integrity and start building and protecting the network you will depend on for your entire career.

Real Networks Versus Customer Relationship Management Systems (CRMs)

CRM systems help manage customer relationship databases for large global companies. You must utilize the system as your company requires. Large, formal and expensive CRM systems must not influence developing, maintaining and growing your network. CRM systems benefit from your networking ability, but not necessarily the other way around. When using a CRM system, always maintain a parallel personal network database backed up at home.

The process of developing direct client relationships is not reliant on or governed by any formal corporate system. For example, if you change employment, you will not take the company's CRM system with you. Still, you will take the network of contacts you brought to the company from your previous work and those you subsequently develop while working at the new company. Theoretically, no one can take this knowledge-based asset from you. You may have to sign a non-compete agreement if you resign, but these contracts are effective for only a reasonable period. Your network and its contact

information are knowledge and is one thing that people cannot take from you. However, as previously discussed, you can physically lose your contact database and you can destroy your network when your reputation and integrity have been severely damaged.

Virtual Networking Considerations

As a business development consultant, I supported my client with an international market development project during the COVID-19 pandemic. The market development plan focused on introducing the company to my network and registering our interest in offering our services to these clients. Our original plan was to travel and meet clients in person, and the itinerary would have included multiple countries, cities and back-to-back client meetings. The trip would qualify as a 'complex' international business development trip. The pandemic changed the original plan and the entire business development process was conducted virtually, providing the experience for the discussion below.

We started the marketing process by sending clients a letter of introduction, requesting a brief virtual meeting to introduce our team and company, which most clients did not know. Introduction and meeting request correspondence had to quickly catch the client's attention to see our company capable of supporting their needs, then agree to meet with us virtually. A poorly written communication is usually not read, and a second attempt to connect with the prospective client might be ignored entirely and no meeting would be secured.

The following points highlight areas I observed as vital to virtual meeting planning and execution.

1. Identification of Correct Client Contact

   Utilizing your direct and indirect network, you must identify the right person(s) within the targeted company to send the introductory email. If the mail does not reach the correct person, it is most likely not read nor forwarded to the proper client representative.

2. Introductory Email Communication

   Keep in mind that the client must first read your email communication. The email should be personalized and concise for this to happen. To personalize the first communications, one option is a reference to earlier events and mutual connections you and the client can relate to. Otherwise, you must research and comment on client activities to effectively personalize communication. The main point is for the communication not to look and sound like one copied and pasted from other client correspondence. I suggest never using boilerplate-type communications.

   Work to present the introductory email in three stages, each effectively taking the reader to the next stage, as follows:

   (a) Email introduction – a concise one or two paragraphs.
   (b) Key bullet points of the Letter of Introduction.
   (c) Letter of Introduction and Corporate Literature.

   The first paragraph of the email should state the purpose of the communication and highlight the communication's goal, for example, formally introducing your company and qualifying as an approved contractor or supplier of services. The client should not have to read the complete communication to determine its purpose.

3. Letter of Introduction and Corporate Information

Drafting an attention-getting Letter of Introduction may take days. The letter will continually evolve and there is always room for improvement. A two-page introduction letter is too long for the client to scan and read quickly. For this reason, you should prepare a short bullet summary of key points of the Letter of Introduction and paste the summary to the bottom of the email. The bullet points must effectively grab the client's attention before they will read the attached Letter of Introduction and other corporate information. I have often made the mistake of overloading the client with information in the introductory communication. Send only the information you feel the client will scan or read, never more. You should always say in the email that there are attachments and how many.

Other Networking Considerations

After working a few years in an industry, it will seem much smaller than was your initial perception. People tend to spend an entire career in the same industry, and over their career, many will have worked for several companies within the industry. People move between companies, voluntarily or involuntarily, but tend not to go too far away. If they do leave the industry, many often reappear after a period. For these reasons, you should maintain contact with those in your network, even if they are not important to your current responsibilities. Most likely, they may again be vital to your business development effort; alternatively, they may be an employment opportunity for you in their new company. Your career will pass too quickly and as your near retirement age, you will see your career as a flash in time. There is insufficient time to lose contact and reconnect with important people in your network. Most importantly, never burn

bridges within your company or industry or fail to be as kind to your subordinates as you are to your superiors.

Equally important is developing an effective arm's length relationship with your competition, who you will meet at industry conferences, trade association meetings, and project site visits for contract bidding and tender processes. My experience is that you should take every opportunity to meet and maintain transparent contact with competitors for several reasons. One primary benefit is that you will better understand the competition's philosophy relative to the projects you both compete for. For example, some competitors may talk openly about their plan to bid or not bid on a high-priority project. This information will allow you to adjust your strategy (and price) accordingly. Also, competitors may not be competitors in the sense that their capabilities may complement yours as they have the technology your company needs and combined, the joint capabilities exceed the other competitors. One more consideration is future employment with the competition should you become dissatisfied with your current employer or leave for varied reasons. Also, your employer may hire the competitor to be your boss or coworker. Having said the above, always maintain an awareness of your industry's perception of your relationship with the competitor. You should keep the relationship transparent and at arm's length.

Industry trade and professional associations are excellent networking resources. Internationally, industry associations and chambers of commerce provide useful local information sources. They will often offer a membership listing, contact information and may assist in arranging meetings during your visit to the country. Regional offices of international consulting firms are also excellent networking and information resources.

The Value of Client - Supplier Trust

'*Speed of Trust*' by Stephen Covey is an excellent read. One primary takeaway from the book is straightforward; you can accomplish things not otherwise possible when you work with people you trust. A trusting client-supplier relationship is invaluable to commercial success. Doing business with people you have a sincere, trusting relationship with is fun and stimulating. Your goal in all client relationships should be to develop long-term client relationships based on trust, for example, handshake agreements. My experience is that trusting business relationships often result in long-term friendships.

Agency Relationships Must Not Replace Direct Relationships

Many international business development and salespeople rely heavily on in-country third-party agents to directly manage client relationships. These agents typically establish a direct relationship with the client and stand between you and the client. All activities are channeled through the agent, who usually is compensated on a commission basis for their services.

Building direct client relationships always results in a more genuine and lasting client-contractor rapport. Unfortunately, I have seen many situations where the business development manager makes little effort to establish a direct client relationship. In some instances, the agents perceive themselves as indispensable to the account relationship. Some agents may not be fully transparent and are too close with the client. These situations create the opportunity for collusion and financial arrangements that deviate from the agency agreement's intentions.

Having said the above, clients in certain parts of the world may require you to utilize a specific agent's services. This should alert you that there may be special arrangements between client personnel and the less than arm's length agent. The main point is closely scrutinizing and monitoring transparency levels for cozy agency-agent-client relationships. Agency agreements should clearly outline the agent's responsibilities and your expectations. Where appropriate, obtain project nondisclosure agreements. Do not let the agent control the client relationship, or 'let the tail wag the dog'. In all agency relationships, always maintain a direct relationship with the client. Be aware of the agent who attempts to discourage your direct connection with the client.

Business Development In-Person Representation and Key Account Management

Many global companies manage ongoing client relationship activities utilizing key account management systems. The company's global client base is allocated among a small group of upper-level key account managers typically based in the company's home office, often overseas and distant from the client bases. It is usually difficult for most global key account managers in larger companies to complete two annual visits to the client's office, international headquarters, or regional offices. Typically, these key account management systems are soon abandoned because the key account managers cannot, or do not, meet with the client as planned. As discussed below, this presents a job security opportunity for the regionally based business development manager.

Clients often have spontaneous project requirements and, absent pandemic periods, they will request an in-person meeting on short notice to obtain input on your company's capabilities to support the project. It is impossible for a key account manager located overseas to attend these meetings on such short notice. These situations create

opportunities for the locally based (or regional-based) business development manager to represent their company at the impromptu client meeting in person and for the key account manager to join virtually. Having your company physically present in the client's office for these impromptu meetings is most effective.

The main point is that global client-supplier relationships are complicated by physical distance and time zone differences. There is no substitute for frequent and regular face-to-face client contact. The regional business development manager is often the best resource to compensate for this weakness in global account management programs. Most importantly, the professional who recognizes these situations and effectively supports the global account manager makes themselves more indispensable to the client relationship. You should continuously look for opportunities like this that secure your position, and at the same time, complement your company's client relationship programs.

CHAPTER 3

Intracompany Team
Communications,
Internal Networks and
Difficult Colleagues

INTERNAL NETWORKS ARE AS key to your success as a robust external network. However, enlarging your internal network simultaneously increases the risk of encountering issues with colleagues who challenge your involvement in their activities for assorted reasons. You must deal with these often career-threatening situations.

Internal Networks

Developing global business opportunities that result in profitable contracts depends on the effective coordination of external and

internal networks. Your internal networks may or may not be in the same corporate division or group; however, establishing mutually beneficial working relationships with geographically dispersed colleagues provides you with an extra set of eyes and ears in their region, 24/7. Select international colleagues can be incredibly proactive supporters of your development activities and are often most willing to assist. Others do not have the broader capabilities or see no personal benefit in supporting international colleagues from other divisions. They may feel threatened and react accordingly. Internal networks and colleague relationships are developed the same way as an external network – primarily a give-and-take approach supported with regular contact.

When traveling in the colleague's country, you should schedule a time to meet, have dinner and explain your business and your potential client base in his country. Likewise, learn more about the colleague's business and how you can support his activities through your contacts. I am aware of many instances where the local colleague's knowledge and local network were not considered in the project development process. No effort was made to connect networks and valuable local knowledge was missed. This should never happen.

Virtual Team Meetings

As an international business development manager, you will plan and coordinate virtual marketing and project development meetings with global colleagues. As discussed throughout the book, the basic principles for planning and conducting virtual and in-person meetings with clients and colleagues are the same, except, obviously, for the need to travel.

Internationally dispersed commercial teams rarely meet in person, making it challenging to develop productive working relationships. To

compensate, one connecting tool is for team members to share a brief personal biography and for you to encourage team members to communicate informally outside formal meetings.

Virtual Team Document Sharing

Documents shared during virtual team meetings are best maintained on a web-based shared drive and be accessible by all participants. Each document's sensitivity and team accessibility must be thoroughly assessed before sharing.

Document organization on shared drives is influenced by team size, industry and team goals. One example of a global commercial team's shared file drive is the following:

Folder 1
1. Business Development Team Meeting Schedules
2. Meeting Agendas (Working Draft and Final)
3. Meeting Notes

Folder 2
1. Client Communications
2. Working Draft of Company Letter of Introduction/Request for Meeting

Folder 3
1. General Industry Information

Folder 4
1   Brownfield Project Data
2   Greenfield Project Data
3   Client Data Bases

Folder 5

1. Company Brochures
2. Company PowerPoint Presentation
3. Company Referenced Trade Journal and Other Articles

Folder 6
1. Customer Relationship Management (CRM)

Folder 7
1. Administrative Matters:
   a. Overview of rules, conventions and use of the shared platform
   b. Team communication modes
   c. Document/file naming
   d. Communication copy distribution, email chain maintenance
   e. Email etiquette reminders
   f. All other administrative considerations for the team to maintain proper communications and manage shared documents

I highly recommend backing up shared files on your PC.

Considerations for Commercial Team Written Communications

The quality of intracompany written communications with colleagues does not require the same formality as with clients; however, such communications must be well-written. Poorly written correspondence with colleagues, such as misspelled words, improper or missing capitalization, and incorrect grammar, yields disrespect and a bad impression.

Assume you send a well-written email that you consider important, but the international colleague does not respond within a

period you consider reasonable. You then assume the email was not read, not regarded as important, or the colleague thought it to be pushy. After a brief period, you want to follow up, asking why they did not respond. Then, you receive a genuinely cordial email stating that the colleague agreed with your communication. The colleague might have been offended if you followed up too soon. We need to be aware that the process for international team communications moves slower because of distance, culture, language differences or not sharing sufficiently close personal relationships as you naturally develop with colleagues in your office. Also, other cultures may be more sensitive to email tone. For these reasons, internal communications with international colleagues should be professionally written.

As the lead person for international virtual commercial team meetings, establish a close working relationship with at least one colleague in each international office location. This contact provides the opening for private communications to discuss team progress, structure, and other matters vital to the team's ability to accomplish the business goals. In addition, a trusted contact can alert you of any team issues before they become problematic and difficult to correct remotely.

All international team members must understand the group structure and their specific responsibilities. Most commercial teams are not formally structured organizations within the corporation; however, preparing and sharing a team organization chart is helpful to all participants.

Job Security, Flexibility and Multi-Division Support

International business development positions expose you to internal and external career opportunities that you would typically not become aware of working in jobs with more limited exposure. A

business development position presents opportunities to work with multiple internal divisions and interact with clients in numerous industry segments. With international business development responsibilities, you will have a close-up view of many current or future career interest opportunities. You will gain a broad base of technical knowledge to support future opportunities.

International business development positions often present career growth opportunities in other corporate divisions. Broadening position responsibilities may also present employment risks. When working with and across multiple company divisions, management teams and global colleagues must view your contributions as team-focused and not self-serving. Your colleagues must see you as the 'go-to' person to support a wide range of their needs. The broad base of business development responsibilities can protect your job from industry downturns; however, as your responsibilities expand, bear in mind that no person is indispensable. If your colleagues feel you consider yourself indispensable, they might view you more as a threat to themselves and less as a valuable team player.

Conversely, if you offer your expertise freely and willingly, your colleagues might view you as a welcome asset and resource in any new project. Collaborating with colleagues from multiple international divisions requires being well-rounded and empathetic to colleagues' feelings towards you. When working with multiple corporate divisions, you must develop a thorough understanding of your activities' benefits to the team, the company and the industry – not just the benefit to you. An international professional capable of working with and across multiple international divisions, in the manner described, is not indispensable but is undoubtedly the right person for a global business development position.

Working from the US as an international business development manager for a multi-divisional European company, to better secure my position, I expanded my internal client base over several years,

from one to four divisions. Still, each of the four divisions was interconnected because they supported client projects at distinct stages of the project life cycle. My multi-divisional position required developing interdivisional networks and becoming technically knowledgeable about each division's capabilities while simultaneously expanding my external client networks.

Representing multiple company divisions solidified my position during tough economic times and was extremely convenient for my company because each division shared my time and cost proportionately. Having multi-divisional responsibilities ensured a high utilization of my available time and required that I continuously prioritize my activities between divisions. For multi-divisional projects, I was often the first person that clients contacted.

My experience is that when meeting with a client to discuss a project focused on one division's capabilities, questions specific to another division's capabilities frequently arise. I learned to quickly switch divisional hats and address the client's question, versus having to say, "that scope of work will need to be covered by colleagues in the other division." Remember that clients see you as representing the company and often are not so concerned about which division you speak for. I quickly recognized that it was necessary to develop the capability to respond sufficiently to first-level questions for each division of the company until I could arrange for the respective subject matter experts to travel and meet with the client to focus on the specific work scope at a more technically advanced level.

Having developed a multi-divisional business development position and responsibility, I protected my job from industry downturns. In addition, being flexible in my work allowed me to reallocate my time to the divisions whose activities had the highest priority. Had I not provided value to multiple divisions, I am sure that I would have been laid off during any one of several downturns. You must be aware of the downsides of the multi-divisional business

development position. In my case, working for four divisions, no one division received over 50% of my time. As a result, I did not administratively belong to a single division, and my cost was allocated to each division based on the approximate time incurred. I did not report to a single divisional manager, for whom my work was concentrated, whom I could rely on for performance reviews, salary compensation matters, or other administrative matters. To compensate for the lack of structure, I needed to establish contact with the executive to whom the divisional managers reported. This worked well until the executive retired. The multi-divisional responsibilities protected my position through the downturns, but after several corporate acquisitions, I did not preserve my job. Working for multiple divisions has both risks and rewards.

Problematic Colleagues

As you grow professionally, assume greater responsibilities and expand your internal network, you will encounter difficult colleagues with whom you must deal. These situations are most difficult to resolve when the colleague is based in another country and you are unaware of their adverse activities because of the distance. You must maintain trusted colleague contacts globally whom you can depend on to keep their ear to the ground and alert you when these matters arise. Conversely, you should provide similar support to your remote colleagues.

You may encounter the following situations, which you must attempt to resolve promptly: A colleague might discredit you, take credit for your work, or sabotage your efforts. Others will intentionally not recognize you for your contribution to a contract award - giving the credit to others. Some will exclude you from important communications with a group of colleagues when you are equally part of the respective group. Others might do anything within their power to see that you are terminated. You may be blamed for a

foolish action or a mistake made by another colleague. These situations can be unpleasant but must be dealt with as soon as you become aware of the problem.

Colleagues create the problems mentioned above for several reasons. They may be insecure in their job or not appreciate your involvement as a business development manager supporting their division. Some may take credit for your work to compensate for their inferior performance; they might be envious of your responsibilities or have other personal problems with you, or they may be protecting another person. You may have been extremely careful to avoid these situations, but they will happen and you must deal with them. As previously mentioned, incorrect and harmful information travels extremely fast with social media.

My experience is that other colleagues and management typically see through most of the situations presented above. Depending on the specific case, you can talk to the appropriate person(s) to find a solution. For others, it is best to avoid them to the extent possible. Take a reliable, respected witness who is not known as your ally if you confront the situation. Before engaging a colleague with whom you have issues, take the time to analyze the situation thoroughly, document the facts in writing, do your best to understand why the individual is acting as he is and consider how you might interact differently with the person. Remember that your goal is not to make the person like you but to demonstrate that you pose no threat but instead support their position or divisional goals. If these efforts are not sufficient, it is time to discuss the matter with a person in upper management who can intervene. Your responsibility is to ensure that issues with colleagues do not negatively affect the project or your career. If you do not take the required corrective measures and the project suffers because of the problem, you may be held responsible.

If you are assertive and proactive in your work, problematic situations will arise at some point in your career, typically as you

advance within an organization and work across multiple divisions. These problems will test your endurance. Never overreact, no matter how correct you may be. To avoid overreacting, slow down, write a response to the issue but do not send it until the next day. Before sending the response, review it, edit it and decide whether it will achieve the desired result.

I know I have overreacted to situations, and I now see this was not constructive in hindsight. Simultaneously, you cannot let people take advantage of you for their self-fulfillment or other motives. How you manage difficult colleague issues is what is important.

Part 2
International Business Development Campaign Management, Planning and Execution

CHAPTER 4

The Complex Trip

THE SUCCESS OF AN international business development campaign depends upon a comprehensive planning process. Initial market development trips typically take a broad market approach to connect with multiple clients, suppliers and others required to develop the market.

Your objective for the first development trip is to meet as many different companies as possible to understand the local market and introduce your company and its capabilities. These first exploratory business expeditions are complex trips because they require multiple client meetings over an extended period, often in multiple cities and countries. Follow-up trips will focus on the higher potential clients and projects identified during the first broader market-focused trip. Planning the first trip, you will identify a select group of targeted clients you envision presenting potential opportunities. There is potential to misidentify some companies' probable value in your broad-based planning and trip execution. Companies initially

considered high potential are often later determined to be low potential; companies initially regarded as having a low value may represent the highest value and opportunity.

For the above reasons, for initial market development trips, maintain an open mind and consider each company as having high potential. Leave all preconceived biases at home and, again, treat each contact as 'high potential'. Working with a full itinerary of back-to-back meetings, the client must not get the impression that you are rushing through your presentation material to get to the next meeting on time. Treat each potential client as your most important prospect, as they very well might be your best opportunity.

Complex Meeting Itineraries versus Single Project Related Meetings

Scheduling multiple, back-to-back, short-duration meetings in multiple cities and countries is much more challenging than is the case for a single client or single project type trip and meeting. A complex business development trip is designed to cover the regional market and maximize the number of targeted client meetings over a fixed period of one or two weeks. Project-based meetings do not require such rigorous schedule management. The focus is typically on a single project with one client with whom you have previously established a working relationship. Project-based meetings are comparatively easier to plan and manage on short notice. Complex trip planning must be initiated as soon as possible, and even then, assume you are short of time because it seems you always could use much more.

Detail Illustration of a Complex Trip

In the Introduction, I defined a complex trip to include a combination of the following elements:
a. Multiple countries

b. Multiple cities
c. Numerous back-to-back meetings (a broad market approach)
d. One week or more of travel

Planning a trip to a country you have never visited and securing multiple meetings is exceptionally challenging. Everything is new to you and you are new to the client. There are no shortcuts for planning a complex international business trip. A big mistake is grossly underestimating the time required to design, build and execute a strategically organized itinerary and travel plan. Gone are the days when one might travel abroad for one or two days of marketing-focused meetings, then fly back home on Friday to enjoy an entirely free weekend with friends and family. In the complex business trip example presented below, you will note that our team had to utilize all the time available to plan and execute the trip. For instance, the travel itinerary scheduled meetings over breakfasts, lunches, dinners and weekends. As a result, travel costs were minimized by covering the market in one trip (versus two trips) and the use of available travel team time was efficient.

The following summarizes the actual planning and execution time for a successful 15-day business development campaign to the South American countries of Guyana, Suriname, Trinidad and Colombia. Consider the following:

Planning Day Range:

Planning Start Date:	July 20
Planning End Date:	September 6
Total Planning Period – Start to Finish	48 days/approx. 1.50 months

Trip Execution Period:

Trip Start Date	September 7
Trip End Date	September 21
Total Trip Days	15 days

"Billable" Time Incurred:

Pre-Trip Market Analysis and Review	9 hrs.
Trip Planning and Organization	53 hrs.
Trip execution time	
(meetings, client meals, logistics)	156 hrs.
Total Direct Planning and Execution	
Time Dedicated to Business Development Campaign	218 hrs.

Itinerary Scope:

Number of Meetings:	35 meetings
Countries Traveled:	4 countries

Results – Business Trip Goals:

All pre-established business goals were accomplished.

Two takeaways from the above time summary are as follow:

1. The total planning time for a complex trip can easily account for 40% or more of the total working hours actually incurred on the trip.
2. The entire planning period range was 48 days, or a bit more than triple times as long as the trip itself.

This South American trip required significant planning for the following reasons, all of which apply to most initial international business development trips:

1. The complexity of the travel plan (multiple destinations and meetings).
2. The weakness of our contact network in the country.
3. The remoteness of the area.
4. Unfamiliarity with the client's operating bases, countries and cities visited.
5. Scope of the project goals.

6. Other complexities specific to the area of travel.

This and the following chapter's overall goal is to guide you in preparing the pro-forma or first draft itinerary that presents the optimum travel plan. A primary planning goal is that the final travel plan does not vary significantly from the initial pro-forma itinerary plan. (I use the term pro-forma in the same manner as for pro-forma financial statements that are intended to approximate actual financial results).

You might call the person responsible for trip planning, management and execution the 'trip manager.' This colleague is typically the business development manager and is the travel team's point person for all communications with clients, management and third parties. Therefore, this information is directed towards you, the business development and trip manager, responsible for the trip's overall success.

Goals of the Trip

First, you must develop clear and concise business goals for each international market development trip. Each meeting is scheduled and all related planning must focus on the pre-established goals of the trip. For the South America trip example, our travel team drafted the following business goals approved by upper management before initiating the planning process. All planning was based on the following goals:

1. To evaluate the potential for our services in Guyana, Suriname, Colombia and Trinidad.
2. To present our capabilities to support the needs of the targeted client companies currently working in the country.
3. To identify and meet with potential joint venture partners capable of providing local content and investment capability.

4. To identify and evaluate the competition.

5. To identify and qualify for appropriate current tenders (or bid processes).

6. To develop a level of knowledge and expertise that would be invaluable to a potential client considering entering the area.

Network Challenges - South America Complex Trip Illustration

For the four-country complex business development trip to South America, it had been several years since I last traveled to Guyana, Suriname and Trinidad. Scheduling targeted client meetings was challenging, even though I had many contact names from these countries in my database. Many of the emails requesting meetings were returned, stating 'address not found' or similar. Realizing that planning and scheduling key meetings for these countries would be difficult, we initiated the planning process six weeks before travel. This time frame was required to design, build and complete this complex four-country trip's travel plan and itinerary. Any less available planning time would have jeopardized the success of the trip.

Identifying, requesting and confirming meetings with targeted clients is always a challenge, especially if your company's first exposure to the country and your network is limited. You must be persistent in securing meetings but not to the point of becoming annoying. This can be a delicate balance. Lastly, you will rely heavily on your internal and external networks to secure meetings.

CHAPTER 5

The Travel Team

Travel Team Management and Leadership

As the international business development manager, you are responsible for planning, managing and executing the market development project. It is possible that you are not the most senior colleague on the travel team. Still, management is aware of your professional growth potential, cultural interests, organization skills and ability to work effectively with others. This is your chance to demonstrate your capabilities and assume full responsibility for the results. Your first responsibility is to ensure that the travel team includes the required expertise for technical presentations and responding to client technical inquiries. The most effective travel team will consist of colleagues who will continue to be involved with the client and the project. The consistency of personnel attending future client meetings is instrumental to the development process,

especially once the meetings focus on specific projects. A former client commented that his impression was that the first meeting with Team A was typically followed up and handed over to Team B. Continuity of competent personnel is vital to building long-term client relationships. This should be considered when selecting travel team members.

Optimize the size of the travel team. A large team is challenging to manage logistically and may be less effective than a smaller unit. A team of one person is too small and is not advisable. Note that only one or two client representatives may attend initial client meetings. A large travel team outnumbering the client's side unbalances the discussion and might make the client uncomfortable.

One other point regarding travel team size and international travel is that you should never attend an international meeting alone. Foreign accents and sometimes their use of English may affect your comprehension. Two team members will have a much better opportunity of understanding the major points of the discussions.

Management Approvals

Your immediate goal as the trip manager must be to receive full management approval to travel. Documents submitted for management approval will vary between companies and may include the following:

1. Business goals of the trip
2. Comprehensive travel plan (or itinerary)
3. Travel budget
4. Travel team qualifications

The trip manager should prepare the first draft of these documents, review them with the travel team, then submit the final

drafts for management review and approval, preferably in a single packet with an appropriate transmittal document.

Managements' formal and front-end approval of the above documents is key to initiating the planning process. Formal management approval will minimize the trip's risk of being delayed or canceled internally after the planning process is well advanced. Managers who may object to the trip will typically be much easier to work with at the planning process's front-end than at the end. The consequences of late-period changes in travel plans are often difficult to adjust for and might jeopardize the trip. Complex trips may be canceled late in the process because planning communications were not shared with specific managers or executives. This can lead to embarrassing situations with clients and subsequent efforts to reschedule the canceled meetings are much more difficult.

Benefits of Early Management Approvals - South American Complex Trip Illustration

For the complex trip to South America, the first drafts of the pro-forma travel plan, travel budget and goals were prepared and sent to the appropriate managers for review and approval. Management's feedback was that a broader base of meetings was preferred in each country and should include discussions with financial consulting firms to obtain necessary information on corporate structure, tax matters and general regulatory and economic knowledge. No other changes were made to the pro-forma itinerary and travel plan.

Having received management's input at the front-end of planning provided ample time to adjust the itinerary to reflect management's expanded expectations and avoided a last-minute rush and potentially expensive changes in the travel plan. Interestingly, management's suggestion to meet with financial consulting firms in each country was brilliant, especially for local commercial and regulatory information

in Guyana and Suriname's developing markets. The financial consultants provided contact information for local companies they recommended as potential partners, who were financially sound and met government-imposed local content requirements. A great takeaway is to always consult global financial consulting firms, especially in developing countries. One other planning consideration before travel is to meet with colleagues who had previously worked in the country, as their experience and knowledge are always beneficial.

Planning Administrative Support

The trip manager must assume and maintain complete responsibility and control for trip planning. It is important not to delegate this responsibility to others. However, solid administrative support is required, especially for complex trips, further backed up by a professional 24/7 travel agent to book and change flights, hotels and coordinate other travel activities on the go. A skilled and dedicated administrative assistant must communicate and coordinate with colleagues in multiple time zones and be available early morning before the office opens, after hours and on weekends. You should stay in close contact with this person and periodically talk by phone to enhance the relationship. Complement the administrative assistant for work well done and ensure that others in your company are aware of their superb performance. These professionals are indispensable to international business travel planning and execution phases and should be treated as project team members.

Professional 24/7 Travel Agents

The added value of a professional travel agent is indispensable to international travel planning and execution. Once you establish a relationship with a competent 24/7 travel agent, do your absolute best to maintain the relationship. Over time, this person will know your

travel requirements inside and out and can be relied on to book the correct airplane seat, order suitable meals, book your preferred hotel room floor and location and much more. As an international traveler, you must have a clear understanding with your travel agent that you will need 24/7 assistance. I have had several outstanding agents over the years, but I never had the opportunity to meet them and thank them in person for their superb work. The travel agency would host an annual customer appreciation reception, but it seems that I was always traveling and missed these opportunities. In hindsight, I now see that I should have taken the opportunity to invite the agent for lunch or send them a gift for a job well done. Always do your best to maintain the services of a single professional travel agent who knows your travel requirements inside and out. If possible, encourage your administrative assistant to meet the travel agent in person, possibly over lunch. These two professionals working closely together are vital to planning and executing international business development trips.

CHAPTER 6

Planning Challenges and Considerations

INTERNATIONAL TRAVEL POSES PLANNing challenges that are not present in domestic travel, requiring strict time budgeting to complete a comprehensive travel plan and depart on time. In this chapter I discuss areas that will consistently challenge available planning time.

Visa Application and Issuance Delays

As an international traveler, you must first assume that visas are required for all countries on the itinerary until you are 100% positive that a visa is unnecessary. Visa conditions are politically driven, the requirements are different for each country and they change often. Therefore, you should never think that visa requirements will be the same as a recent trip to the same country. Utilizing the services of a professional passport company is highly suggested for determining

visa requirements and expediting the visa application and issuance process. These companies typically provide, free of charge, country visa requirement information.

The visas application process must be started as soon as possible, but never later than a decision has been made to travel. It is important to remember that you will be without your passport while the visa is being processed, which may be a week or more. The processing time will depend on the country of travel, the consulate's location and available consulate staffing for processing the visas. Expect delays in processing visas during pandemic periods. All other international travel must be scheduled around the absence of your passport unless you have a second passport. The visa process can be further complicated for several reasons, including country requirements for formal letters of invitation from your international host and official letters from your company guaranteeing fiscal responsibility for your trip. If available, always request expedited service from the passport and visa service professionals for an additional cost.

Most visa applications will require a copy of your flight itinerary and always multiple passport-size photos. Therefore, you should always carry an ample supply of passport photos, which tend to be used rapidly. If required, a travel agent can prepare a 'dummy' flight schedule to apply for the visa, which is another reason to have a working relationship with a professional travel agent. Visa processing delays include immigration office backlogs, delivery delays, temporarily misdirected passports, the availability of managers in your office or the international host's office to write and sign letters of invitation or fiscal responsibility.

Should the visas not be obtained before travel, some countries will issue the visa upon arrival or have an online visa application option on their website. The airport visa issuance process can take hours, typically requiring waiting in a lengthy line at 2 am in an unairconditioned customs office and an annoyed, overworked

immigration agent. Therefore, arriving with a valid visa in your passport is always the best choice.

A multiple entry visa is highly recommended if available and if there is a chance you will return to the country. Some countries, such as Brazil, India and others, offer multiple entry visas for extended periods. Multiple entry visas are most important to those who must travel on short notice, such as emergency response personnel. Having a multiple entry visa will allow you to be on the next flight out.

Time Zone Challenges

A second planning challenge often overlooked by the trip manager is the number of common office hours you will have with colleagues and clients in different time zones. For example, if you are based in Houston and your travel team is in the Netherlands, you have only approximately two hours of common workday time for direct real-time communications, depending on regular office hours. On the other hand, some colleagues may have flexible working hours, and on Fridays, they arrive at their office early to leave work early for the weekend. In this case, you have only four days or eight hours per week of common workday time. The same considerations apply to communications with clients in other time zones. Time zone differences constantly challenge and shorten available planning time and must be considered when estimating the time required to complete the planning. Further, the hybrid work models resulting from the COVID-19 pandemic have further complicated the common working hours for colleagues in other time zones.

Virtual Meeting Planning - Electronic Calendar Invitation Advantages

Virtual meeting platforms, such as Zoom, Microsoft Teams and others allow the meeting organizer to schedule and request meetings using an electronic calendar, such as Microsoft Outlook. My preference for requesting introductory person-to-person meetings is via a formal email or letter, depending on the importance of the meeting and the invitee's required formality level. Once the meeting is confirmed, follow up with an electronic meeting invitation.

The electronic calendar invitation is most convenient for scheduling meetings with clients and colleagues in different time zones. The calendar invitation meeting time set for your location will automatically adjust meeting times on invitee invitations to their respective time zones. There is no need to calculate the meeting time in each recipient's time zone, which can be difficult because some countries adapt to/from Daylight Savings on different dates, while others do not change during the year. Most countries in Africa and Asia do not observe daylight saving time, nor do many countries close to the equator.

I recently scheduled a virtual meeting with attendees in five different time zones. The client was in Norway and asked that the meeting be scheduled at 17:00 in Rio de Janeiro to accommodate his Brazilian colleague's schedule. Using the International Meeting Planner's website www.timeanddate.com, I determined that my local time for the meeting was 14:00, based on the 17:00 Brazil meeting requirement. On the Zoom meeting invitation, I set the meeting time at 14:00 and relied on the electronic calendar invitation to properly adjust the meeting time to each recipient's different time zone. Not physically seeing each attendee's invitation received, I am always concerned that time zone adjustments might not be correctly reflected on their invitation. I am also worried that invitees might travel to different time zones before the meeting date, and their

electronic or personal calendars, for whatever reason, do not adjust the meeting time for their new time zone. To ensure that all attendees have the correct meeting time, you should also send a note at the bottom of the electronic calendar invitation stating the meeting time in Universal Coordinated Time ('UTC' - formerly referred to as GMT). There is no reason for invitees to be confused about or not know the correct meeting time in their physical time zone. Further, from recent experience during the COVID-19 pandemic, sending reminder emails is often necessary on the morning of the meeting. This may seem like overkill; however, the number of clients or colleagues who had recently confirmed the meeting and had forgotten about the appointment is incredible.

Meeting Scheduling Advantages of Early Planning

The early front-end stages of the trip planning are the only time you will have complete control of your itinerary and the client meeting order and times. The pro-forma itinerary represents the perfect meeting sequence and is not initially influenced by the client's proposed meeting dates and times. My experience is that clients fully appreciate and understand that you are making a significant financial and time investment to travel and meet with them in their country. If you start planning well in advance of the travel date (i.e., four to six weeks), clients will generally make their best effort to block out sufficient time on their busy calendar and they will do their best to keep the meeting date and time you first request. The early meeting request will also increase the client's ability to arrange for the appropriate personnel to attend. Equally, early planning best ensures that your travel team includes the technical expertise required to present capabilities to respond appropriately to clients' inquiries.

Planning Challenges- South America Complex Trip Illustration

My client's first exposure to South America was the primary planning challenge for the complex, four-country trip to Guyana, Suriname, Trinidad and Colombia presented in Chapter 4. My networks in three of these countries had not been fully maintained for five years, and contacts had either left the country or were no longer suitable relative to our business goals. It was as if this was also my first trip to these countries.

The second challenge was that planning and approvals had to be completed during August for an early and fixed September travel window. August is the typical vacation month for many people in Europe and South America. As such, many of the targeted clients were on holiday, as was the case for my European travel team members and our divisional managers. There was no flexibility in travel dates, so the challenge was to manage the delays and uncertainties caused by people's unavailability during the heavy planning period.

The third challenge was that one of the four countries had exceptionally cumbersome visa requirements and required letters of corporate financial responsibility for each travel team member and a formal letter of invitation from a host country client. Five years ago, I traveled to the same country and the visa requirements were then quite simple. However, you should never assume that visa requirements are unchanged from previous trips. As previously noted, visa requirements are often politically motivated and can change frequently. We were fortunate to have sufficient planning time budgeted to obtain the required information.

Host Country Customs and Considerations for Planning

Many countries have numerous national and religious holidays. A pro-forma itinerary cannot be prepared without knowing whether the intended travel dates are during a holiday. The prospective clients may take an extra day of vacation on either side of a holiday. A plan to travel during a week that includes a national or religious holiday will not be an optimum week for your trip. If a holiday falls during the workweek, many countries will move the holiday to the following Monday. Merely knowing the holiday's date is not enough for your planning. You may find yourself enjoying the holiday as well, which is a terrific way to get closer to the local culture but may not provide the time you would like to spend with the clients.

Preparing a pro-forma meeting itinerary requires knowing the host country's customary office hours, lunch and dinner schedules. If the country uses a 24-hour military time system, you should request meetings utilizing this system. I suggest you adopt the 24-hour time system, which I find preferable for itinerary preparation and much less confusing internationally than the 12-hour AM/PM system. Many countries have work hour customs significantly different from the US and Europe. For example, in Mexico and Argentina, a meeting at 18:00 in the client's office is perfectly acceptable. If the plan is to meet for lunch or dinner in these countries, a 15:00 or 16:00 lunch and a 20:00 or 21:00 dinner is typical. In these countries, an early morning meeting may be at 10:00 and certainly nothing much earlier. I attended a meeting in Paraguay with the Energy Minister at 23:00. In 1960, Che Guevara met with Julio Lobo, 'Sugar King of Cuba', at midnight to discuss the future of sugar in Cuba after the Cuban revolution. Even Lobo, a Cuban, thought that was an odd hour to meet.

It is important not to schedule meals or meeting times based on your home country's customs. I have seen colleagues and others request client lunch and dinner meetings at the time they eat at home.

Such requests are inconsiderate to the host country client and demonstrate inflexibility and a lack of host country cultural knowledge.

Meeting Time Control and Logistics

It is important that the itinerary and meeting agendas present meeting start and finish times and fit within the client's time allocation. Any considerable time overruns should be because of client interest in your company's capabilities and not your lack of organization. Significant meeting time overruns on a packed itinerary will always snowball and all subsequent meetings for that day will suffer as a result. For this reason, try not to overload your daily schedule with meetings. Time overruns caused by client interest and questions, not your poor organization, are encouraging. Work to build sufficient time into your itinerary for meeting time overruns to the extent possible. If additional meeting time is required, ask the client if it might be possible to schedule a second meeting while in the host country.

Limiting the number of daily meetings to one in the morning and one in the afternoon will protect the itinerary from time overrun issues. For most initial complex business development and marketing trips, a full schedule of back-to-back meetings is often required to cover the market within the available number of trip days, as was the case in the South American trip example. This said, never cut short a productive meeting with a prospective client with a potential business opportunity, as you might an appointment with a supplier, consultant, or advisor, for whom you are the client.

A client once told me that one of the worst impressions new suppliers can make in introductory meetings is rushing through the meeting to be on time for a second meeting with another client company. Do not give the client the feeling that you are on a fishing

trip. Treat each prospective client as if they are the only company you are meeting with on the trip. Client companies talk with each other about suppliers and their capabilities. Leaving a wrong impression with one client can spread to other companies within the industry.

Try to leave one day free on your itinerary if you have the luxury, preferably the last day. My experience is that this day will be effectively utilized to follow up on opportunities and schedule additional meetings you become aware of during your trip. In addition, the free day is used for preparing meeting reports, responding to emails, returning phone calls and much more. If possible, add an open day on the pro-forma itinerary for these purposes or simply use the time to explore the city. The free day is, without a doubt, a luxury to the international business traveler.

Meeting logistics and travel time considerations must be considered when developing the pro-forma itinerary. The itinerary must provide enough travel time between meetings. On a map, office locations may look close to each other; however, severe traffic congestion is common in most large international cities. Clients in these large cities usually understand traffic delays; however, in most countries, it makes a good impression on the client by arriving at their office a few minutes early. Therefore, any foreseen delay should be immediately communicated to the client.

Budget enough time to register with the client's security desk, watch the company's safety video and in some cases, take a test on the safety presentation. I have seen situations where this process required more than half an hour. If given one, keep the safety clearance card documenting that you have completed the safety course. Otherwise, you may be required to retake the course on your next visit.

Importance of Separate Airline Ticket Booking Records

When traveling in remote parts of the world on multiple airlines, to the extent possible, discuss with your travel agent the advantages of booking each leg of the trip as a separate record versus a single ticket record. This also applies to leisure travel. For certain airlines in developing parts of the world, having individual records will simplify any flight segment changes. Flight record issues that we experienced in the past have been significantly reduced with interconnected global airline computer reservation systems. This matter should be discussed with your travel agent.

Meeting Attendance Insurance

For meetings vital to the business goals such as contract negotiations, ensure that your team's key people will be in-country and attend the meeting. This can be accomplished by splitting the team into two flights and sending the most experienced persons for the project on a separate flight a day or two in advance. What can go wrong with international flights might go wrong, and splitting the travel team-up will best ensure that you have representatives at the meeting. If you had the foresight to divide the team, a canceled or severely delayed flight because of weather or mechanical issues will not completely torpedo the meeting.

Planning Relative to a Commitment to an International Career

International business trips typically require a 24/7 commitment with long days and nights on airplanes, meetings, meals, moving between meetings and short nights in hotels. Longer flights and connections may take 15 to 30 plus hours of the total door-to-door travel time over multiple time zones. You must strive to arrive as

rested as possible to be effective and you must plan to spend enough time in-country to accomplish the trip's business goals.

I have been on complex trips where travel team members wanted to depart from home on a Sunday evening or Monday morning and return home by Friday for the weekend, regardless of the time required to accomplish the business goals. International travel is typically spread over a reasonable period throughout the year. As such, the travel plan should provide adequate time in-country to achieve the business goals and this often requires flying on the weekend and returning on the following weekend or the next week. In a post-pandemic era, we may no longer have the luxury of flying in and out of a country for a short stay as many did in the past. Most of us will have to plan to stay abroad for sufficient days to complete the plan in one trip. Do not rush the trip and try to arrive as fresh as possible to adjust for the time changes. Many people are severely affected by jet lag for varied reasons. For example, I often cannot sleep on long flights, promoting jet lag. Each of us are affected differently and must deal with the situation in our own way.

Arriving on the weekend, a couple of days before your meetings allows you to adjust to the time zone, get to know the city and mix a bit with the local culture. Take the time required to get your feet securely on the ground. Your company may, or may not, pay for the extra weekend hotel nights. Usually, airfares and hotels are discounted if you stay over a Saturday night. The extra day or two in the country provides the opportunity to recover from jet lag and learn more about your host country. Looking back on my travels, I should have spent more personal weekend time exploring the host cities of the world's areas that I traveled, even though I often returned on leisure trips. Your host country contacts will also appreciate your interest in learning more about their culture, city and country.

My client in Argentina was shocked that I attended a Sunday afternoon Boca Junior and River Plate football (soccer for the

Americans) match. I was even more surprised than them that I returned safely from the match and was at work on Monday morning. It was a fantastic cultural experience and a tense match, a weekend that I will never forget. Further, on a recent trip to Guyana, our clients were remarkably impressed that our travel team took the time on a weekend in their county to attend their favorite sporting event, cricket. It was another fantastic cultural experience that certainly beats staying in the hotel and something to chat with the client about at dinner. Clients appreciate contractors and suppliers mixing with their local culture. Extra time in the country is instrumental to the overall business development process, connects you with the client and the local culture, and is enjoyable!

Home Departure Checklist and Managing Other Non-Business Matters

You will not enjoy the trip, concentrate and function well if you are worried about matters and things at home that you cannot manage after you have departed. Having personal issues in order at home, to the extent possible, is vital to your ability to achieve your business goals. In Tool No. 6, I share a copy of my home departure checklist, which you can modify for your needs. You will notice that the checklist includes simple things to do, but each of these items has the potential of disrupting the business trip, such as making sure cookstove burners are all off, lights and water are off and more. My wife and I habitually turn off the master water valve to protect against a broken pipe flooding our house while we are both traveling. I know of more than one incident of people traveling outside the country who received a message from a neighbor stating that water was pouring out from under their home's front door.

These concerns will affect your ability to concentrate and perform while on a business trip. You will be more worried about what is happening at home than your business responsibilities. These

situations always are most magnified when you are far from home for an extended time and you feel helpless to do anything to address the problem. Prepare a comprehensive home departure checklist to ensure that things are in order and that incidents at home do not negatively impact your business trip. For any personal issues, do your best to address these matters as well as possible before departing.

CHAPTER 7

Itinerary Construction

THE ORDER OF MEETINGS for a complex trip is key in achieving the business goals, and information obtained from one meeting ideally supports the following. This chapter highlights the value of early preparation of the pro-forma itinerary and trip plan to ensure trip success best.

Itinerary and Travel Plan Preparation

Your itinerary should be a single, comprehensive-stand-alone document that includes all planned trip activities and supporting information from start to finish. Necessary itinerary details will consist of the following:

1. Well-designed document indicating draft date and time.
2. Travel team names, contact information and medical alerts.
3. Business goals of the trip.

4. Travel agent and office support contact information.
5. Flight information and schedules.
6. Meeting schedules, key contacts, address and contact information.
7. Restaurant and hotel reservations, contact information.
8. Logistics details, including team meeting points/locations, transport details and contact information.
9. Agendas, equipment and materials required for each meeting.
10. Maps.
11. Any other information you consider key to the trip.

The itinerary is effectively the perfect map for the trip - a continuous schedule of daily activities from home departure through return - meetings and activities for each day, breakfast through dinner. A well-written and regularly updated itinerary is the primary tool for managing the trip: the larger your travel team, the higher the level of itinerary detail. Integral to the plan's effectiveness is the timely electronic sharing of itinerary updates with your team using a group messaging platform. Updated itineraries should also be provided to office assistants, travel agents, other colleagues, select managers and family members. (See Tool No.1 for an example of a pro-forma itinerary).

Significance of Pro-forma Planning

The pro-forma itinerary represents the ideal plan to accomplish the trip's business goals. The goal is for the final executed itinerary and the original pro-forma itinerary to be similar. The trip manager drafts the plan that reflects optimum travel dates, the most efficient travel logistics and a meeting and travel sequence that flows in a manner that supports an orderly gathering of information to achieve the business goals. Early planning minimizes late-stage changes in trip planning.

The trip manager will prepare a pro-forma itinerary as follows:

1. Prepare a list of targeted clients and other preferred meetings for each country and city.

2. Prepare a daily meeting schedule for each city, scheduling client meetings in an optimum order that best supports business goals. The more important meetings should be scheduled near the end of the week, effectively utilizing knowledge learned in less important meetings at the beginning of the week. As the week progresses, you will also gather relevant information regarding the competition, potential partners, suppliers and local knowledge. Such information is often most valuable to the meetings scheduled at the end of the week.

3. Ensure that the week of travel for each country does not coincide with a major national or religious holiday or other events that will restrict client availability for meetings, such as a well-attended industry conference inside or outside the country. During in-country industry conferences, the client is typically inundated with visiting suppliers requesting appointments.

4. The draft pro-forma itinerary determines the travel days and dates required to realize the optimum order of meetings.

5. Immediately communicate the pro-forma itinerary to your travel department or travel agent to determine if airline flight schedules can support the pro-forma travel plan.

6. Initiate visa process.

7. Based on the travel department's report on flight availability, adjust the pro-forma travel itinerary to accommodate available flights.

8. Promptly book provisional flights (cancelable & changeable tickets) for the entire travel team, flying from multiple locations globally.

9. Once provisional flights are booked, begin formerly requesting client meetings based on the pro-forma plan.

10. Do not overschedule daily meetings. Instead, allow for time overruns, unplanned meetings and sufficient free time for administrative duties, emails, and more.

The above steps should be modified as required for each trip.

Template of Pro-forma Itinerary

One means of expediting the overall planning process is to prepare a pro-forma itinerary template in anticipation of future travel– with dates not yet known and travel not yet formally approved by management. Assume that the ideal pro-forma travel plan for a trip requires a minimum of five days of consecutive back-to-back meetings. You prepare in advance a five-day pro-forma meeting itinerary (i.e., Monday through Friday with no dates set at this time). This pro-forma itinerary will save considerable time when the exact travel dates are later confirmed. Since flight schedules usually are the same for each week, suitable flights can be inserted into the pro-forma itinerary template. The itinerary can be completed quickly once you get the go-ahead for travel, book the flights, initiate the visa application process and schedule client meetings.

Pro-forma Itinerary Construction - South America Complex Trip Illustration

Our preliminary analysis of the South American trip presented in Chapter 4 concluded that the information obtained in Guyana would be useful to the meetings we planned for Suriname. Data from both countries was vital to the Trinidad meetings. The reverse order of first visiting Colombia and Trinidad would not have supported the Guyana and Suriname visits' goals. This illustrates that planning the optimum logistical order of travel and meetings may be vital to achieving the trip's business development goals.

Most importantly to note for this trip, it would have been impossible to realize the preferred order of country visits had we not initiated travel planning one and one-half months in advance. If this country travel sequence had not been achieved, it would have required two separate trips to execute the travel plan. In our case, two trips were not an option. Sufficient planning time is cost-effective and maximizes the use of valuable in-country time.

Optimum Trip Length

My experience is that travel team productivity starts to decline rapidly after one week (10 days maximum) of multiple back-to-back, international meetings on a complex trip. Nevertheless, the distance, remoteness of the countries and travel costs may dictate a full one or two-week travel plan, as was the case for the complex trip to South America that I use as an illustration. After a week of multiple back-to-back meetings, the team will tire, your minds get mushy and meeting details start to run together. For maximum productivity, try to schedule a one-day break between a series of meetings.

Importance of Early Flight Planning and Confirmation

My experience is not to begin requesting client meetings until after travel is formally approved by management, flight availability is confirmed, and flights are provisionally booked. Flight planning must be extremely high on your travel action list, on the same level as securing visas. After preparing the first draft of the pro-forma itinerary and travel plan and there is a reasonable probability that the trip will be approved, coordinate the pro-forma itinerary with a professional travel agent to determine if flights are available for all team members to support the travel plan. Promptly book travel team member flights with flexible/changeable/cancellable tickets. This point is paramount for trips to remote areas of the world where flights are limited, especially when colleagues are traveling from multiple international locations. Flights to the cities on the itinerary may have limited schedules, or flights may be entirely overbooked. If the required flights are not available, you will have to reorganize and adjust the country travel order accordingly. Logistical issues are minimized if the travel team is booked on the same flights.

Early Flight Planning Challenge - South American Complex Trip Illustration

The complex trip to South America was full of flight planning obstacles caused by not promptly booking available flights early in the planning process. The only control you have over flight schedules is to book available flights before they are filled. At the beginning of the 48-day planning period, I prepared a pro-forma itinerary that scheduled the optimum country visit sequence and the optimum number of meeting days in each country on the itinerary. The executive assistant in Europe immediately coordinated the pro-forma itinerary with the travel agent. Fortunately, at that time, flights were

available that perfectly supported the pro-forma itinerary and travel plan; however, they could not be booked without executive approval.

As previously noted, planning for the South America trip was initiated in late July for the scheduled September travel window. Late July and early August are the primary vacation season in Europe and managers from whom we needed final travel approval were on their family holidays. As a result, the executive assistant could not obtain the required management approvals to book the (then) available airline tickets for the flights necessary to accomplish the pro-forma trip plan.

Several days had passed before the executive assistant received the final approvals to book the flights. Unfortunately, after this delay (six weeks before the planned travel), two previously available flights, both key to the overall trip plan's logistical order, were no longer available. Thus, to realize the pro-forma itinerary's travel order, we would lose two workdays on the itinerary because of flight schedule changes. This required taking indirect flights through Panama, requiring two full days of travel not initially planned. Nevertheless, we maintained the required logistical order of counties to visit, but we had less time in-country than budgeted initially.

The following email correspondence from the administrative manager in Europe further highlights this issue:

European Office Manager:

"Also, we are facing a small issue, since the flight on the 13 September is not available anymore and the only option is travel on the 14th 09.00, but your plans for Cartagena will fall apart. Is there any room for adjustment? Please let me know, as we will issue all tickets to prevent this happening to other flights as well. Please let me know what we can do about the change from the departure of Suriname."

I take the time to present the detail above to demonstrate the importance of booking available flights immediately on a provisional, refundable and changeable basis. Furthermore, this example illustrates how flight booking delays and any oversights can have a snowball effect and potentially tank the trip.

When trip planning is initiated early on, you still have time to adjust to flight schedule changes that otherwise will challenge the overall trip planning.

Pro-forma Itinerary Updates

The developing itinerary must clearly indicate the status of meetings requested and confirmed, including dates requested and confirmed. My experience is that the easiest way to record and control meeting requests correspondence sent is to type on the itinerary: (Meeting Requested 1 August 2021), (Second Request sent 8 August 2021). Write out the dates. In the US, we place the month before the day (8-1-21), and in other parts of the world, the day comes first and the month second 1-8-21). Otherwise, your colleagues in other parts of the world may be confused by the date format.

As itinerary items are confirmed, I highlight all confirmed information on the itinerary in **Bold Print** and add details such as:
- **Meeting Confirmed – 15 August 2021**
- **Hotel Confirmed – 16 August 2021**

Every item on the itinerary in **Bold Print** indicates that it is confirmed, including:
- Flights
- Hotels
- Restaurants
- Car service

Any bolded item does not need to be considered again in the planning process unless reconfirming the item. All items should be periodically reconfirmed and written as:

-    **Reconfirmed on 20 August 2021**

All itinerary items that are not bolded represent incomplete items, those open or outstanding, or need the stated further attention. You and your colleagues will benefit by not needing to read every item on the updated itinerary to determine the current planning status. You may have your preferred method of controlling the development of the itinerary. The above process has worked well for me.

CHAPTER 8

Client Communications and Other Trip Planning Considerations

It is important to invest the time to ensure that all client communications are concise and grammatically correct. The extra time is always less than the time required to correct errors and miscommunications.

Meeting Agendas

Preparing a well-thought-out agenda for each meeting is an effective tool for advancing communications with the client regarding the subject matter, attendees, and much more. Formally prepared meeting agendas may not be customary in many parts of the world,

where meetings are often, intentionally, less structured. However, on a complex international business trip, you may have multiple short meetings each day and important agenda items must be completed in the time the client has allowed. For countries where the agenda may not be commonplace, you should communicate to your host that you understand formal agendas may not be common in their country but would appreciate using this tool to best use the client's time. Be clear in communications that you will adapt the meeting length to fit the client's busy schedule. The meeting agenda is a good organization and time control tool and will help the client choose appropriate attendees.

A complete agenda will state the meeting objective and list all attendees and their titles. Confirm with the host who will introduce client attendees at the start of the meeting. The client should introduce their team first. To the extent possible, each agenda section should indicate the name of the person responsible for presenting each item, with a suggested start and finish time listed. Often the meeting will not precisely follow the agenda, but it is a valuable tool to estimate if enough time is allocated to each item. It is best to move the most important topics up on the agenda to ensure that these items are discussed.

The meeting agenda may be used to communicate other information to the client and their administrative assistant regarding any special equipment requirements for the meeting. These items may include a projector, sound system for a corporate video, or assistance in making copies of certain documents (i.e., the meeting agenda) for the attendees. After confirming the meeting, the draft agenda should be sent to the client for review and input.

The agenda is a fundamental outline of meeting items to be discussed. In preparing for the meeting, prepare a template of detailed items for each item on the agenda. As the meeting progresses, occasionally glance at the template to ensure that you have covered

all the items listed. Using this approach, you and your team will be well prepared for the meeting, all items will be discussed or considered, and the information will help prepare the meeting minutes. (See Tool No. 4 and 5 for examples of meeting agendas for in-person and virtual meetings.)

Well-Written Client Meeting Request Communications

All client meeting request communications, emails and formal letters must be concise and grammatically correct. The first communication introducing your company to an important client and requesting the initial meeting should be written with the same care as writing a CV cover letter to a prospective employer. Client communications should compel attention and respect in every conceivable way. You need to communicate the professionalism and experience that drive your company in a limited number of words. Well-written communications will improve the client's probability of reading the message and responding.

In many cases, you may have only one opportunity to reach the client and it must be right the first time. Having to rescind extremely important communications because of a misstatement or other correspondence errors is embarrassing and unnecessary. Never believe that you can 'recall' a poorly written email message – it does not work. I have spent hours drafting meeting requests. Letters discussing sensitive or confidential matters must be approved by management and must be perfectly written. When preparing sensitive communications, you should develop the habit of writing the first draft, putting it down for a day or two and then re-reading and revising. You will always make needed changes to the communication's tone, grammar, or the entire direction of the letter. It is best never to rush sensitive or otherwise important emails or letters.

One more consideration is when a traditional and formal form of correspondence is more appropriate than a basic email. I suggest writing a formal signed letter and pasting a PDF copy to the body of the email for these situations. By sending a formal and personalized letter instead of an email message, most clients will understand that you consider your communication important and will typically read the letter. A compelling message must be written specifically for the client - not a copied, pasted, or modified communication that you have used for other client communications. Otherwise, the client will immediately discern from the communication's tone that it is not explicitly written for them. (See Tool No. 3 for an example of a client meeting request.)

All emails sent should ask for a 'Request Delivery Receipt' and a 'Request Read Receipt'. Returned emails must be resolved accordingly. For emails that appear to have been sent to the proper address, but no reply has been received from the client, wait a few days, then resend the same email with a brief note asking if the client may not have seen it, hoping that they will respond to the second email. Enough time must pass before sending a second request to those who have not responded, as you never want to appear to be desperate or pushy in requesting meetings.

Planning Correspondence Control

Complex trips will invariably involve hundreds of email communications, and I find it helpful to file all related correspondence electronically in a single trip folder. To maintain a complete file, I go to Sent mail and the Inbox each day, dragging all associated emails to the respective trip folder. This correspondence folder is handy for planning future trips.

Meeting Reconfirmation

Approximately one week before travel, reconfirm all appointments with the clients by email, stating that your travel planning is on schedule and that you and your team look forward to the meeting. It is also important to reconfirm the meeting a day or two in advance, as many clients may not have recorded the meeting on their calendar or may forget. This is a compelling reason to send an electronic calendar invitation after the meeting has been confirmed.

You will typically have several email communications with each client before establishing a final meeting date and time. You may feel that the number of communications is excessive; however, this is not unusual in organizing meetings where you and your company are new to the client or schedules are continually changing. Subsequent client meetings will require much less correspondence as you will be recognized and better known by the client.

A complex trip itinerary will continually change throughout the planning and execution phases. The travel team manager must be fast thinking and agile to manage last-minute itinerary changes, especially while traveling. They must adjust the plan quickly and in a manner that best supports achieving the business goals. A test of planning agility is when clients request a last-minute change in meeting time or location or a change in the meeting subject content at the last minute. Unfortunately, sometimes, meetings are canceled at the last minute.

Guidelines and Considerations for Client Introductory Communications

As I previously commented, when writing to multiple clients to introduce your company to request a virtual or in-person meeting, there is often a tendency to save time by modifying similar communications sent to other clients versus writing an entirely new personalized communication. This is extremely risky and the

potential for error is extraordinary. Furthermore, the tone of these communications will always come across to the client as a canned-boilerplate message and not uniquely written for them.

The following points, many previously discussed, apply to all client communications:

1. <u>Personalize Each Communication</u>

   The safest policy is that each client's communication is independently drafted and not modified by a previously sent communication. Start clean and fresh.

2. <u>Write, Review and Rereview All Correspondence</u>

   Freshly drafted client communications will transmit a much-needed personal tone that will not otherwise be achieved. One suggestion is first to prepare the message in a Word, Apple Pages, or other word processing file document; then spell and grammar check the draft, set it aside for a while, then reread it. You will frequently change the message's wording and tone after letting the language sit for a while. Once pasted to the face of the email, reread and grammar and spell-check once more. One-day delay in sending is ideal. I realize this sounds excessive, but the extra time you incur will be much less than the time required to correct poorly written communications sent.

3. <u>Test Download All Attachments</u>

   Before sending the email, test download all the attachments to ascertain that you have attached the correct documents and that they will properly download when selected or clicked on by the client.

4. Double Check Email Account Used

If you use several email accounts, ensure that you send the introductory email using the correct business email account and not a personal account or an email address you use for other employers if you are a consultant.

5. Refrain from Forwarding Emails

First, remember that forwarding any email is dangerous and presents a risk of passing confidential or embarrassing information to others. When you must forward an email to third parties, double-check the information at the bottom of the email and all attachments and ascertain that it is not confidential or otherwise should not be sent to a third party. Drafting emails from scratch always prevents this issue from happening.

6. Colleague Reviews

Have other colleagues review the correspondence.

7. Email Addressing

Lastly and extremely important, do not add addresses to the email until you are fully prepared to send the email, as emails are easily unintentionally sent. Double-check the correctness of the primary addressee and the appropriateness of all persons copied.

Now you are ready to send the email.

The above guidance has worked for me and is generally commonsense. Preparing, updating and consistently following your email communications checklist will help minimize the embarrassing

errors we all make. The process for ensuring that client correspondence is well-written may seem painstakingly slow and tedious, but the extra time is worth the investment, and in the end, will save time. Over my career, I have made every error imaginable when sending emails because I was in a hurry to communicate. Take your time to read, reread, double-check – triple-check all external communications.

CHAPTER 9

Client Meetings

THE FIRST MEETING WITH the client presents the opening opportunity to interact face-to-face or virtually and formally and introduce your company's capabilities to support the client's project needs. My experience is that the initial meeting will typically be short, around 1 hour to 1.5 hours for an in-person meeting and approximately 30 to 45 minutes for a virtual meeting. Client attendance will vary depending on the overall level of interest in your company's capabilities and client representatives' availability. A broad base of attendees from multiple disciplines is always encouraging. A client-approved agenda will provide the basic structure for the meeting. The client representative you coordinated the meeting with will typically continue as the primary company contact during the early development phase. This person will open the meeting, introduce your company and their team's attendees, then give you the floor lead. You will then proceed with the agenda. Meeting time will pass rapidly and you must be well organized and prepared to cover

the introductory material and respond to client questions in a minimal amount of time.

Basic Principles for Conducting All First Client Meetings - In-Person and Virtual

Before reviewing the components of the introductory client meeting, I will first highlight several basic principles that should govern your team's performance during the meeting, be it in person or virtually:

1. First, it is important to recognize that the client is extremely busy and has provided you with valuable time for the meeting. The agenda must be concise and highly focused on the client's needs. Think of the first meeting as an audition or a screening that your company must pass before the client provides you longer meeting times, should you be invited back.

2. Your team must recognize that the client is an expert in their field and all discussions, interactions and presentation materials reflect this point.

3. It is important to remember that the client accepted the meeting because they see your company as having resources or capabilities required to support their needs. Presentation material should focus on the client's needs, with minimal time spent on general corporate information, which can be sent to attendees before the meeting or shared after the meeting.

4. Before attending the meeting, your team must thoroughly understand the client's operations and business needs. Such information is typically available on the client's website, industry periodicals and other resources. Team members should never ask questions during the meeting that indicate no effort has been

made to research client information and background or project information. Instead, they should ask questions and make comments suggesting that they have done their client homework. In addition to general corporate information, review the principal client representative's biography and background, often available on LinkedIn.

5. Team questions should be scripted to the extent possible. Team members attend the meeting principally to answer questions, preferably directed by the team leader. Unscripted comments by team members unintentionally may leak confidential information from another client.

6. Your team should always include subject matter experts capable of fully responding to clients' technical and operational questions. Never bluff and always promise to answer with considered opinion after consulting with experts within your company. Follow up promptly, preferably within 24 hours, before momentum is lost.

7. Remember that the client's first meeting often determines the relationship's future. For this reason, the front-end time investment in meeting planning and execution is important to the process.

8. The introductory meeting is not the venue to present your or any of your team's personal achievements, awards, and extensive experience resume. Remember that the client is interested in your company's capabilities - not your team's background and accomplishments.

Presentations must be concise and to the point. If you can professionally cover the material without a PowerPoint presentation, hats off to you. In place of the PowerPoint presentation, demonstrate your respect for attendee intelligence by handing out, or virtually

sharing, a suitable reprint of a technical paper on the subject matter authored by your company. It will be refreshing and memorable to the client. PowerPoint often bores clients, and one often hears clients comment about 'Death by PowerPoint'.

For virtual presentations, my experience is that a PowerPoint presentation of no more than two or three perfectly prepared slides is ideal. Presenting the slides in 10 minutes or less provides more time for client interactions and discussions focused on the client's needs.

The introductory meeting is often the product of weeks or months of focused networking, client communications and market research. You will never feel that you have over-planned for a client meeting, but you will always regret being ill-prepared. Being well-prepared increases your overall confidence level, visible to the client and is reflected in overall team performance during the meeting. Notably, the client will quickly notice your level of confidence. Conversely, poor planning and organization may compromise your company's initial impression and capabilities to support the client's needs.

The following discussion is focused on four components of the client meeting and provides general guidance for the travel team.

Pre-Meeting Preparations	Meeting Execution	Meeting Etiquette	Post Client Meeting and Other
✓ Presentation	✓ Presentation	✓ Meeting	✓ Minutes of
✓ Equipment	Content	Attire	Meetings
✓ Backup	✓ Presentation	✓ Mobile	✓ Client Follow-
Presentation	Delivery	Phones	Up Meeting
Capability	✓ 'Reading' the	✓ No	Frequency
✓ Pre-Meeting	Audience	Unnecessary	
Client		Side	
Attendee		Discussions	
Interactions		✓ Listen	

✓ Meeting Agenda		✓ Cultural Mannerisms ✓ Political Questions ✓ 'Loose Lips Sink Ships'	✓ Follow-up Client Communicatio ns – Unilateral Requests to Send Information ✓ Elevator Pitch Presentation ✓ Always Carry your tool bag

Presentation Equipment

If time permits, arrive at the client offices 20 to 30 minutes early to set up, test presentation equipment and ensure that you have all presentation information well-organized on your computer's desktop and ready to go. Try not to search around your laptop during the presentation to find the correct files. A client told me that when he sees his guest supplier select all presentation files from a single folder named Client X Meeting, he knows that the presenter is well-prepared for the meeting. Ascertain that any application media that might pop up on the screen during the presentation, such as email and other notifications, are turned completely off. I have seen too many embarrassing pop-up messages appear on the presentation screen for all to see. One was an email from the client's primary competitor, and another was an embarrassing message from a girlfriend. Close all computer applications you will not use for the presentation and eliminate the risks of embarrassment and other distractions that might negate an otherwise effective presentation. The safest policy is to disconnect from WiFi and the internet during your presentation.

For virtual presentations, the same procedures for in-person presentations apply. Pre-presentation testing of the video camera,

microphones, speakers and files to be shared is vital to the meeting's success, as you are 100% dependent on the technology. Correcting a technical issue may use valuable client meeting time and participants may log off and not return to the meeting. For in-person and virtual meetings, have a second backup presentation and other information loaded on a second-team member's computer and ready for presentation should the first option fail. Continually evaluate presentation technical risks and have more than one backup plan.

For IT security considerations at in-person presentations, larger companies often require you to use their computer systems. You will need to have the presentation and any additional information pertinent to the meeting available on a thumb drive. Otherwise, you will connect your computer to the client's projector, so be prepared for either approach. During the planning phase, communicate with the client regarding the presentation plan and ask if a projector will be available for your use. In the more remote areas of the world, you may need to bring a portable projector. Not so many years ago, hardware incompatibility was common before video standardization. In many countries, companies may not have a projector available for third-party use. Communicate all meeting equipment needs in advance. The meeting agenda working draft is an excellent tool for these communications.

If the presentation includes a corporate movie with sound, ask the client if you can use their sound system in advance. Client audio systems are often technically challenging to connect to and must be tested before the meeting. In addition, if a video or movie is important to your presentation, consider bringing small external computer speakers versus using the often-inaudible built-in laptop computer speakers. Ask the client if IT assistance will be available should any issues occur with the presentation equipment.

Backup Presentation Capability

What can go wrong with electronic equipment, projectors, computers and other presentation equipment will go wrong. In Argentina, starting my presentation, I plugged my laptop computer (dual 120v/220v capability) into the electrical outlet. There was a power surge, a loud pop, sparks and that was the end of my computer, as well as the end of my PowerPoint presentation. Always bring a backup copy of your presentation on a thumb drive and keep a copy remotely in cloud storage. You should also carry a presentation hard copy, which if required, can be copied in the client's office and distributed to the attendees. Another option is to maintain presentation backup copies on your company logo thumb drives. These give-away thumb drives are always appreciated. The thumb drive can also include copies of corporate brochures and other bulky information, which there will not be sufficient time to present during the meeting.

Pre-Meeting Client Attendee Interactions

One principal advantage of arriving and setting up early is that this provides an opportunity to meet and briefly chat with client attendees before the meeting starts. As attendees arrive, circulate the room, introduce yourself and exchange business cards. By greeting attendees as they enter the meeting room, you will typically have the opportunity for a brief period of informal one-on-one contact. When exchanging business cards, take time to respectfully look at and read the card before putting it into your pocket. As a speaker or presenter, my experience is that I am always much more relaxed when I have previously met and briefly chatted with attendees. Consider placing the attendee's business cards on the table in front of you to reflect their position around the room. This practice will help you remember attendee locations in the room and assist in addressing them by name - an excellent tool for connecting with your audience.

Meeting Agenda

The client-approved meeting agenda prepared during the planning phase will guide and control the meeting and best ensure covering all items in the allocated time. This said, always remember that you are the guest and the client controls the meeting. As the travel team lead, you should set the tone and casually keep the discussion flowing according to the plan, as any substantial meeting time overrun will affect all subsequent meetings scheduled for the day.

Presentation Content

Your presentation's primary purpose is to reinforce your company's capabilities and experience for supporting the client's project needs. The presentation must focus on a limited number of points that demonstrate your understanding of the client's requirements and your company's ability to provide the best solutions. The best means of maintaining presentation focus is first to prepare two bullet point slides - one listing client needs and the second outlining how your company will fulfill those needs. Information presented between these two bullet point slides should focus on examples and stories that support how your company will accomplish those needs. Always focus on facts that can be confirmed and remember that the client has most likely also done their homework on you.

Your presentation should not be the PowerPoint show. The presentation should be your verbal communications and interactions with the client audience. The PowerPoint slides are simply a tool that supports the oral presentation that you make. Your company may have a long and fascinating history that you feel is important for the client to know. You might even have an elaborate corporate video highlighting the unique corporate history and project successes, complete with upbeat or dramatic music. If your presentation covers

this history and background in detail, presenting this information will reduce the time available to discuss items specific to the client's project needs. The bigger the client, the more you will need to focus on the project, not the client. At the opening of your verbal presentation, clearly state to the audience that you understand their project needs, and that is where you plan to spend meeting time. Then, state that additional information regarding your company's overall capabilities and history will be available after the meeting. You should always focus on the client's needs in the hour you have. Remember that the client probably already knows your company; otherwise, you would not be invited to the meeting.

Your company's public relations department may prepare a generic and comprehensive corporate presentation covering excruciating details such as financial results, corporate history, past projects and current capabilities. These PR department presentations usually include well over 100 to 150 slides, an excellent inventory from which you can use specific slides if required to respond to a client's question. This massive slide inventory should be kept readily available during your presentation. Organize these slides and become familiar with the slide locations to minimize time searching for a specific slide if needed. Most importantly, never use the corporate presentation as a basis for preparing your presentation, even if you radically reduce the number of slides. In my career, I have seen, too many times, these full-blown corporate presentations used as the core presentation with no effort on the presenter's part to prepare a properly focused and customized presentation. I have also seen colleagues use the same presentation previously given to another client, only changing the client's name on the title page but failing to remove the previous client's name from slides inside the presentation. How would you, as a client, feel about this lack of supplier preparation? The title or first slide should personalize the presentation with the client's name, date and location. The title should also provide the audience with a general idea of what you plan to convey in the presentation, for example, "(Your Company's)

Credentials for Providing Guyanese Local Content for Client Project X."

PowerPoint presentations are typically the reason for meeting time overruns. To complete the presentation within the time allowed, the presenter must practice presenting and timing the presentation. Importantly, time should allow for question and answer (Q&A) time, preferably after each slide or area of discussion, instead of at the end of the presentation when the audience may have forgotten what piqued their interest during the slide presentation.

Consider the following additional points for PowerPoint presentations (certain items are discussed in other areas to accent importance):

1. Clients despise long and unfocused PowerPoint presentations. Yet, they often see hundreds of these presentations from suppliers and internal colleagues annually. So, if you use a PowerPoint, it should be different, concise and focused.

2. Ask yourself if a PowerPoint presentation is even necessary. The audience will respect your knowledge of the subject matter when you present without a massive hoard of slides. Instead of looking at the slides, the audience will be looking at you. The communications without PowerPoint will be more direct and much more effective. You can always tell the client that you have prepared a detailed presentation that will be made available after the meeting. It is important to emphasize that the presentation is not the PowerPoint; the presentation is your team's verbal communication of your understanding of the client's needs and how your company is the best option to satisfy those needs.

3. When projecting and presenting slides, stand near the screen so that the audience can simultaneously make eye contact with you and the screen. Best to move around a bit and not hide behind a

podium. Never deliver your presentation sitting down. A proper level of enthusiasm is best projected when you are standing or moving about when appropriate.

4.   Graphic communications should not only include PowerPoint slides. Professionally printed graphs, charts and other media will add variety and effectively communicate important points. Handouts are effective.

5.   Minimize slides that are busy and wordy. Always use bullet points. Each point should be extremely well-written clearly express the point made - practically standing on their own. Avoid using long sentences, and never read the slides to the audience. The attendees should not need to split their attention between the graphic, the screen's text and what you say.

6.   Omit slides with animation unless necessary. For example, bullet points are best presented without using fly-in animation.

7.   Spell and grammar check all slides. Search each presentation for other client names that may be unintentionally left on the slides from prior presentations using the 'Find' function.

8.   All slides should be high quality and primarily consist of photos and possibly a few meaningful charts and graphs.

9.   Always be sufficiently prepared to deliver the presentation information without the aid of PowerPoint. Technical issues might interrupt the presentation, or the client may suggest an open subject matter discussion replacing the PowerPoint presentation due to limited available time. You must do your homework, know your material inside-out and be overly prepared. If you have prepared notes, try not to use them.

10. Without dumbing down the audience, the presentation delivery should use simple words, short sentences and clear pronunciation, yet speaking in a normal tone at an average speed. Relative to word selection, Mark Twain would say, "Don't use a five-dollar word when a fifty-cent word will do."

11. Refrain from jokes and other forms of humor, but do smile often. These points apply to all audiences, in-person or virtual, but especially to an international group whose primary language is not English.

12. Do not use a laser pointer unless you highlight a particular direction of flow, a function or area. Instead of listening to you, the audience's eyes will be following the moving laser.

13. Having a travel team member who can present in the client's language is invaluable. When planning the meeting, confirm the audience's English proficiency with the client and consider using dual languages on slides. Additionally, use the client's system for weights, measurements, currency and date formats in all media.

14. Before the presentation, brief the travel team presenters on how you may interact with them during their presentation, such as 'speed up, slow down, skip that bit or let's discuss that point in more detail'.

Corporate movies and videos usually are professionally prepared and present a comprehensive overview of the company. Considering that the meeting should focus on the client's specific needs, a corporate video may not be appropriate for the core meeting unless specific to the client's project. Should you feel that the video is important information to share with the client, one option is to ask your host if you might present it after the meeting for those who may have a few extra minutes. This offer further demonstrates your recognition of the value of the client's time.

Presentation Delivery

I previously suggested taking the opportunity to meet, greet and briefly talk with client attendees as they enter the meeting room, presenting the chance to establish more meaningful personal connections. As a result, you will find yourself looking more directly at those you previously met and talked to when you are delivering the speech or making the presentation. These brief encounters will help relieve any speaker-related tension. The presentation effectively continues the initial brief and informal discussion you started before the meeting. Everyone has their method of connecting with their audience during a presentation. The above approach has worked well for me, especially for a large audience.

Reading and Interacting with the Audience

How you interact with the client and your ability to pick up on their reactions will lay the foundation for your future relationship with the client. As you deliver the presentation, watch your audience closely and gauge their interest level in the subject matter. If you see people looking at their mobile phones, nodding to sleep, or worse, one by one, slowly leaving the meeting, you know that you must pick up the pace and modify your approach. The team leader must keep the meeting running according to the agenda while a second-team member takes meeting notes and prepares the minutes. A third team member should be responsible for scanning the client attendees and noticing varying signs of agreement, disagreement, or confusion, then feeding this information to the team as required, either during the meeting or afterward.

When presenting your company capabilities, you must be knowledgeable of the client's business segments and be sharply aware of your presentation's areas that may conflict or compete with the client's business. Presenters must read the audience and demonstrate a high sense of empathy. Unfortunately, while making presentations

to key clients, I have seen executives fail to sense the client's adverse reactions to comments made during the presentation that conflicted with the client's business. The executive presenter continued ahead at full speed. This person demonstrated a severe lack of empathy skills, which resulted in significant problems with the client. When presenting, we must be continuously empathetic with the audience.

Minutes of Meetings

You should designate one person with good listening and writing skills to take notes and draft the meeting minutes. High-quality minutes of meetings are dependent on timely preparation. Waiting to write the minutes days after the meeting, or worse, after you return home, ensures all vital information is not incorporated into the document. You will always be delighted with the ease of preparation and the quality of promptly prepared minutes. I have heard managers attending the meeting comment: "from these minutes, I don't think that we attended the same meeting." Avoid this embarrassing situation by following the suggestions above.

Trip Report

My experience is that a comprehensive trip report is most easily prepared using the final trip itinerary file as a template. The trip itinerary and travel plan include all the base information for each meeting: dates, company names, attendees and much more. To this template, you can easily add bullet point notes of the meeting as recorded in the minutes. This approach facilitates and simplifies report preparation and is in a form that is familiar to the travel team.

Receiving business cards from all meeting attendees facilitates meeting report preparation. You can sort the cards in the same order as the itinerary, photocopy them and attach them to the final trip report. In addition, the notes you have made on the back of the

business cards received are handy for preparing minutes and the trip report. As with the minutes, trip reports should be updated daily.

Client Follow-Up

One mistake frequently made in international business development activities is a long-time delay in client follow-up, sending a draft of the meeting minutes, or following up on action items. Regardless of how productive or unproductive the first client meeting may have been, always follow up in writing with the client as soon as possible. Make these communications while traveling or shortly after arriving back home.

You may feel that the meeting was a failure with respect to the goals of the meeting. Clients may not see your capabilities fitting their current project needs. Still, they may be impressed with your overall presentation and the general impression made and will later contact you regarding a completely different project opportunity. This is why the preparation and delivery of each client interaction are so vital to the business development process. Conversely, if the client feels that minimal effort was invested in your meeting preparation, there will be less chance of considering your company for future projects.

Regular and frequent client follow-up visits are the key to international relationship development. I have seen colleagues execute successful international business trips and fail to make regular follow-up trips and visits. The time and cost invested in the initial client meetings were wasted. It is impossible to develop a proper relationship with a global market and client by only making annual visits to the country. To create real opportunities and relationships, you must make regular follow-up visits within a reasonable period following your first complex development trip. Follow-up appointments with companies that do not yet present imminent commercial opportunities will be more simple 'courtesy calls' (and

you can refer to them as such to the client). The follow-up meetings can be very brief and do not require formal presentations but simple updates to maintain the relationship. The idea is to stay in front of the client. Remember, 'out of sight – out of mind'. Over the years, I have learned that most clients will take the time for a brief follow-up meeting, knowing that you will respect their time by keeping the meeting short. On the contrary, if you request an hour or more appointment and ask to make another PowerPoint presentation, the client may not accept the invitation, jeopardizing the opportunity for future follow-up meetings. Always respect the client's time and they will typically accommodate your request for brief and to-the-point follow-up meetings.

The Missing Presentation

My company was invited to develop a Latin American national oil company project. I spent the entire week preparing for the meeting, finishing at 17:00 on the Friday before the Monday meeting in Latin America. I placed the presentation, brochures and other information in a box then asked our office services assistant to lock the material in my car while I closed my office. I soon arrived at my brown Ford Explorer, looked in the windows and the box was not there!

I looked across the parking lot and saw an almost identical colored Ford Explorer, and the box was locked inside. Using my key, I unlocked the car and recovered the presentation material. What are the odds of my key fitting another Ford Explorer of the same tan color? A Google search indicates the odds were 1 in 50,000 for all Ford Explorers. For one of the exact color, the odds had to be infinitesimal. Late on a Friday, the car's owner could have easily driven away by 17:00 with the presentation material. It was highly possible that I would not have noticed that the box was missing from my car until I had left for the airport on Sunday evening for the flight to Latin America. It would have been too late. I would have been wildly

embarrassed to be meeting with executives of a Latin American national oil company without a presentation, brochures, and the other presentation materials I would use to support my company's capabilities for the important project.

This event happened before we depended so heavily on laptop computers, internet cloud storage, or a thumb drive backup. Technology is much more advanced today and maintaining backup presentation files and related materials is much more straightforward. I share this story to illustrate how seemingly impossible circumstances can destroy a trip; all the time, cost and effort invested in trip planning and preparation can very easily be lost. You can never over-plan or over backup materials and information needed for a client meeting.

CHAPTER 10

Team Etiquette and Unique Meeting Options

DEVELOPING INTERNATIONAL RELATIONSHIPS WITH other cultures requires that the travel team's conduct and mannerisms are acceptable to the other culture, are not offensive and do not detract from the relationship-building process. This chapter discusses several areas I have noted as important to etiquette and building relationships in international meeting environments. I also discuss non-traditional meeting options I have found to be highly effective.

Meeting Attire

The business dress code for large international cities is typically formal - dark suits, white shirts and ties. Outside of the major cities,

climate and the local culture influence the dress codes. Determine the companies' dress codes and pack accordingly. If the code is unknown, play it safe by overdressing, then dress down once you see that your host and other client representatives dress less formally. The same goes for lunches and dinners. Always remember that you can always dress down, but not up. If you arrive at the meeting and your host is not wearing a jacket or a tie, take your coat off and consider removing your tie. Dressing down is a considerate gesture that will make the client feel more at ease, especially at a lunch or dinner meeting. I have traveled with colleagues who would not dress down to the client level, as they stated that they were from Country X and it is their home country custom to wear a coat and tie at client dinners and meetings. This attitude shows poor cultural flexibility.

Virtual meetings are typically more informal; however, we must dress appropriately. Even though we are seated in these meetings, it is sometimes necessary to get up from our chairs to take care of various matters. Therefore, you should be appropriately dressed from the waist up and down for virtual meetings. It is always good to turn off the video before standing up.

After landing, you may go directly to a meeting, so plan to arrive dressed and ready. Our colleague arrived at the airport for the flight wearing a gray hoodie sweater and gray gym workout sweatpants. We assumed that his travel gear was for his comfort on the flight and he would change into his business attire on arrival at the host city airport. We were short on time for our first meeting on arrival, so we then assumed that our colleague would change clothes in the client's building lobby restroom. However, he followed the rest of our team to the elevator with the plan to change in the client's restroom. A very formally dressed executive stepped out of the same elevator upon arriving at the client's floor. It turns out that he was the CEO with whom we were to meet within minutes. He knew who we were without question, and he certainly saw our colleague dressed in the sweatsuit. Enough said – we were embarrassed. Always dress

appropriately, even on flights, because you never know who is on the plane. First impressions are lasting. Consider bringing several fresh shirts and look sharp when traveling in hot climates. Use the hotel laundry service daily.

Mobile Phone Etiquette

How many times have we read or heard. "Please silence your mobile phones" in meetings, movies and conferences? I attended a live BBC podcast recording at Rice University in Houston, which celebrated the 50th anniversary of the Apollo 11 lunar moon landing. The program was a fabulous interview of NASA Apollo 11 flight directors and two of the spaceship's astronauts. Before the program began, the producer asked the audience of 75 to 100 people to turn mobile phones off not to interfere with the live podcast recording. Five minutes into the recording, two phones had rung. The BBC commentator had to stop recording the interview for each sounding. He again asked to turn all phones off.

For each interruption, a woman sitting in front of me shook her head in a sign of disgust and she then turned around looking at the person whose phone had sounded. The podcast recording once more resumed, and unbelievably, the phone of the woman who was so irritated by the prior incidents emitted a five-second loud alarm before she could turn it off. These interruptions were very embarrassing to everyone and especially to her. The point is never only to silence your phone in meetings but to turn it entirely off. Some phone alarms and Amber Alerts will sound when the phone is in silent mode. Always ask your travel team to turn their phones completely off in client meetings, both for in-person and virtual meetings. Before the above incident, I only silenced my phone, but I now turn it off.

The following is another phone usage matter for the travel team to consider. A smartphone is a useful tool for taking notes, but in a

meeting, if the client sees you typing on your phone, it may appear to them that you are texting or responding to an email and are not interested in the discussion. Therefore, if a team member must use a notes app on their phone, clearly state to the host that they are using the phone to take notes. However, it is best not to use your phone in any manner in a client meeting. In some countries, it is common for client attendees to receive and make phone calls during the meeting and maintain a loud, open and disruptive conversation. If this happens, continue with your discussion and presentation, but ask your team not to interrupt the meeting with phone usage.

No Side Discussions

The travel team manager should reiterate the importance of not conducting side conversations between colleagues during the meeting unless such discussions are necessary to respond to a client inquiry or similar. Such discussions may give the client the impression that you are unprepared. A travel team composed of subject matter experts allows the team leader to engage the expert to respond to the client's question, eliminating the need for any side discussions that would exclude other meeting attendees. If a detail needs immediate attention, ask for permission to step out of the meeting room and briefly discuss the item. Today's travel teams are often comprised of colleagues from around the world who speak multiple languages. Before all meetings, I always ask my international colleagues not to use their home language to communicate during meetings. The client may misinterpret that the reason for communicating in a foreign language is to discuss confidential or other matters that you do not want the client to understand. They might also think the information is intended to be deceptive. For meetings conducted in English, side discussions in other languages will only create suspicion from the client regarding the subject matter, especially in contract negotiation meetings. Having said this, there are situations where two colleagues can best discuss technical issues in their native language. When it is

necessary to switch languages, one of the involved colleagues should first ask the client host for permission, as follows: "Excuse us, but the subject matter we are discussing is highly technical. Could my colleague and I briefly discuss this subject in Spanish?" The client will then feel more comfortable with the Spanish language side conversation. It is also acceptable to say that the subject matter is quite technical and ask if you and your colleague could step outside the meeting to discuss the topic in your native language and not interrupt the meeting. These requests are signs of openness and transparency and are typically well-received and will build trust with the client.

Lastly, never criticize or disagree with your team members during a client meeting. Unfortunately, many of us have seen colleagues argue about a point in the presence of a client. If a colleague makes an incorrect statement and no one catches the mistake, consult with your team after the meeting and then communicate the correction to the client as soon as possible.

Listen

The meeting agenda must provide sufficient time to listen to and interact with the client, not just present. I have seen situations where my colleagues talked excessively, and when the meeting was over, we did not know any more about the client or project than before we arrived. We must share the available time with the client and never interrupt others. Lastly, always face the person speaking, the client or your colleagues. This is especially important in Asian cultures.

Data Transmission Courtesies to Clients

One more comment indirectly related to etiquette. Never send or 'dump' a large amount of information on a client via email or post without first asking the recipient for permission. Sending a large

amount of data, such as a financial report or similar data, is much less likely to be read if you have not previously asked for their approval to send the information. Dumping information unexpectedly on a client or your CV to a potential employer may also be considered inconsiderate or discourteous. Having the other party first agree to receive the data cuts the dumping issue and politely transmits the information. You are competing with many people for the client's or potential employer's attention and time; your communications must stand out from the crowd to be read.

Lunch and Learn Meetings

Lunch and Learn meetings are an efficient use of client time for introductory, first-time meetings. Clients like this approach because it minimizes the time they and their employees are away from office responsibilities. The planning process is like other meetings, except arrangements are made for a working lunch to be delivered for participants to enjoy during the presentation. My experience is that attendance will typically represent a broader client interest level. I have had Lunch and Learn meetings at major engineering firms attended by 25 or more people, several attendees not in my targeted group, and later presented project opportunities. Lastly, Lunch and Learn meetings will always attract a few attendees looking for a free lunch.

Clients are now accustomed to Lunch and Learn meeting requests and have arrangements with sandwich shops and restaurants to deliver the meal and set up for the luncheon. All you must do is provide the client's office services team with your credit card number. Companies typically limit the number of Lunch and Learn presentations per year.

The Breakfast Meeting Option for Busy Execs

A unique option for meeting with an exceptionally busy client is to request an early breakfast meeting. Many executives in my industry start their workday incredibly early. An early breakfast meeting is an effective option for meeting with these busy executives and managers. In my hometown of Houston, several restaurants cater to early business breakfasts. Many of the restaurants' customers are regular patrons typically found at the same table each morning - the restaurant is their early morning office. The early business breakfast is not so typical in other countries. My international colleagues are always impressed to start our itinerary with a 06:30 breakfast meeting with a key client. Having an early start provides an opportunity for a full day of meetings, especially when the meeting schedule is complex and includes lunch meetings, after-work drinks and dinner meetings. In a pinch, I have scheduled seven appointments in one day, which I do not suggest.

The 'Elevator Pitch' Presentation

I arrived at the client's office and my host very courteously and apologetically said, "We just became aware of an operations emergency that we must deal with immediately. We are not sure if we will be able to reschedule our meeting while you are in the country. Could you quickly tell us about your company in two minutes or less?"

You must always be prepared to present your company quickly, on an impromptu basis. The best means of being prepared is an 'elevator pitch'. The term assumes that you are required to communicate a very concise overview of your company and its capabilities to a third party on a 60-second elevator ride or approximately the time it takes for you and the client to ride from the ground floor to the destination floor. Fortunately, I had memorized my elevator pitch and delivered it in less than two minutes.

Delivering an impromptu verbal presentation in two minutes may not be too challenging for a company with a single divisional activity. However, for a diversified global organization that you had planned to present to the client in a one-hour meeting, it is a self-test to explain in two minutes unless you practice. Nevertheless, my elevator pitch presentation was a success, as the client later rescheduled the appointment for the next day. Therefore, I strongly suggest you write and memorize an elevator pitch that clearly and rapidly presents your company and its capabilities to support client's projects. The client will also be impressed by your organization, flexibility and preparedness if you also give them a thumb drive that includes your presentation, corporate brochure and other pertinent information.

Most colleagues in large and multidivisional companies can present their division's capabilities in two minutes. However, my experience is that most are not sufficiently familiar with other divisions within their company to communicate the information in an elevator pitch effectively. The client sees you as representing the broader company and expects you to have general knowledge of your company's overall capabilities. All employees, not just commercial groups, should memorize a comprehensive corporate elevator speech ready to present at a moment's notice. Imagine how impressed you would be if you cold-called on a company, intending to talk to anyone available who could briefly meet with you and to leave your business card and a corporate brochure. Assume no managers are available and you are directed to the executive assistant, who has memorized an informative company overview that she shares with you in a few minutes in a conversational tone of speech. I know that I would be highly impressed with the executive assistant and the company's overall culture, whose non-commercial employees carry and can professionally share this knowledge about the company's capabilities. Progressive CEOs promote a total team approach to business development, sales and marketing, reflecting that all employees have a sales and business development mindset.

Always Carry Your Tool Bag

A colleague asked if I would join him at a client meeting. He understood that the meeting was with one client representative to discuss a project in West Africa. We arrived at the meeting room, and to our surprise, 15 client representatives from multiple divisions were seated and waiting for us. They were expecting a full-blown corporate capability presentation for their project. My colleague brought a single brochure but no laptop computer and no corporate presentation. I had been retired for over two years. Fortunately, I carried my laptop, on which I had a copy of a short corporate presentation. I quickly added the client's company name and the current date to the first PowerPoint slide, as if we had prepared it especially for this group of 15. It would have been embarrassing not to have the appropriate information to present to the client group. The lesson here is always to carry a corporate presentation, as well as an inventory of corporate slides and other marketing information on yourself, your computer and a thumb drive. You never know, so always be prepared to avoid finding yourself in the compromising position that my colleague experienced. It is also a good idea to carry a copy of your CV on your thumb drive. You never know when a currently updated CV might be needed!

CHAPTER 11

Cultural and Geopolitical Considerations - Explorer Personal Skills

YOU ARE ATTRACTED TO an international business career for many reasons, but one underlying force is a compelling interest in cultures, history and geopolitics. This chapter presents vital points and stories that will help boost your confidence when working in other cultures.

Personal Library Tool

Building a geographic and multi-culture-focused library is enjoyable. A personal library is a most enjoyable means of developing an advanced level of expertise in culture, geography, geopolitics and history for the places you travel. Resale bookstores are an excellent resource for building a focused international subject library at

reasonable prices. My library includes books that reflect my primary geographical areas of interest, Latin America and Africa.

Three books on my shelves I recommend for the international business professional are *The Culture Map – Breaking Through the Invisible Boundaries of Global Business* by Erwin Meyer (Meyer, 2014), *Prisoners of Geography – Ten Maps that Explain Everything About the World,* by Tim Marshall (Marshall, 2015) and *Kiss, Bow or Shake Hands* by Terri Morrison and Wayne A. Conway (2nd ed. 2015). *The Culture Map* uniquely presents a series of country-specific models. Each graphically depicts how each culture views, manages and processes different business and social scenarios, clearly showing areas of similarity or divergence by country and culture. Likewise, *Prisoners of Geography* effectively presents the world in a geopolitical context in ten maps. As the title indicates, *Kiss, Bow or Shake Hands* is a guide to proper international protocol. A series of country and city-specific books that I enjoy and find helpful when preparing for an international trip is *Culture Shock – A Guide to Customs and Etiquette,* published by Graphic Arts Center Publishing Company. Collecting and studying books such as these will elevate your geopolitical and cultural interests and knowledge and will reflect in your performance.

Cultural Adjustment Period

Initial contact and interactions with multinational colleagues and clients require a cultural adjustment period, which will go through various phases of irritation or tolerance until the relationship becomes more open and relaxed. It is important to know that the intercultural adjustment process is normal and will occur.

Traveling internationally soon after September 11, 2001, was often challenging, especially as an American. While traveling with an Italian colleague in Algeria, through Egypt to the UAE, I sensed that he was nervous traveling with an American in that part of the world so soon

after September 11. We had an eight-hour layover in Cairo, Egypt, during a sky-darkening dust storm, like those I remembered growing up in the Texas Panhandle. Tension in the airport was high because of Bagdad's military fall that morning. TVs throughout the airport loudly broadcast the news and the people shouted in protest. The dust storm penetrated the airport lobbies and complimented the tense atmosphere perfectly.

Egyptian immigration took possession of our passports upon our arrival in Cairo and placed all 50 transfer passengers in a small, stuffy, hot and dusty holding room. All were Middle Eastern except my Italian colleague and me. A small black and white TV sat on a chair in the corner of the room, continuously rerunning the video of Iraqis ripping apart Saddam Hussein's statue, followed by an American tank pulling the statue to the ground. People in the airport shouted and cursed the US. The tension was so intense that one could have cut the dusty air with a knife.

My colleague and I could do nothing except sit quietly, keep our heads down and stay busy reading or working on our laptops. At salat, the prayer time, the people covered the entire dirty floor with newspapers and mats to pray. There was barely enough space for all the people, primarily men, to kneel on the floor. Sitting in the middle of the small room, we continued working on our computers, heads down. My computer battery lost power and my Italian colleague asked me what I would do. I said, "I am going to unplug that TV (which was loudly trumpeting the news) and charge my laptop." He believed me, and I saw in his face that he was fearfully startled by my comment, intended to be a joke. (See later comments on joking.) I quickly apologized and explained that I certainly was not serious. He just then understood that I was only trying to make the very tense situation slightly lighter. From that point forward, our relationship was outstanding. We now have known each other for many years and can laugh about the situation; however, he was genuinely uncomfortable traveling with an American during that challenging time in the Middle

East and the world. My suggestion of unplugging the TV confirmed his fears.

A prime takeaway from the story is that I should have been more empathetic and open when I first met my colleague at the beginning of the trip. I should have confirmed that I fully understood the tenseness of the geopolitical situation and atmosphere and said upfront that I would be extremely cautious and intentionally not do or say anything foolish that might create a security issue. For sure, I know that my colleague would have appreciated an open discussion at the beginning of the trip instead of in the middle of all the commotion in the Cairo airport, just after the American tank had pulled down Saddam's statue.

The above story illustrates the importance of understanding that a period of cultural adjustment with colleagues and others is normal, and this must be recognized and discussed early in the relationship. International relationships are dependent upon a high degree of empathy, openness and trust. Traveling globally, you may find yourself in the wrong place at the wrong time, and this is certainly not the time for inappropriate jokes causing undue stress with others, as was the case with my colleague.

People worldwide are friendly if you are kind to them and do not say anything inappropriate. There are no appropriate situations for derogatory comments that might create a security issue if made to the wrong person. In these situations, keep your head down and wait for things to cool off – as was the case in Egypt - do not unplug the TV broadcasting the horrible news to charge your laptop.

Cultural Comparisons

Ernest Hemingway said when visiting other countries, "*You are not supposed to like things. Only to understand.*" Inexperienced

international travelers sometimes openly make host country – home country comparisons of food, dress, religion and anything that diverges significantly from their home culture. Refrain from these comments unless they are positive. Equally, you should never criticize your own country in front of foreigners as this might make you appear untrustworthy and ungrateful. Others may be perplexed at your criticism of your own country or government.

When working with other cultures whose political philosophy, religion and cultural habits are different from yours, I find it beneficial to remember that they did not choose the culture they were born into. Understanding this fact helps me understand them better. One other point to consider when communicating with diverse cultures: I have heard English speakers negatively comment about the broken-imperfect English used by others, knowing that the person commenting spoke only one language. At least the person communicating in imperfect English was fluent in at least another language and most likely more! Consider this point before evaluating another person's accent or flawed use of English.

Nationality Labels

We must use the correct names and references for the geographical areas you travel to and know the geography sufficiently well not to make improper geographical references or labeling. For example, when talking to your Latin American host, you must understand that people from Canada, Mexico, Central America and South America are all Americans. The American continent includes 35 nations and 25 dependencies or non-self-governing territories, and they are all American. If you are from the United States, you are North American, and Mexicans and Canadians are also North Americans. South America has 13 countries; however, it is interesting to note that many South Americans will usually exclude Guyana, French Guyana and Suriname when listing the countries on the South American

continent because these countries are not 'Latin' in their culture. Studying the geography of the areas we travel to helps us make sense of and appreciate the different cultures we work with globally. Learning about our host country's land, its resource availability, and how those have shaped the culture to be the way it is today helps us understand its uniqueness.

Many in the United States do not have passports. This amazes my European friends and they often joke about this reality. The US is a geographically large area, and for many, there are no business reasons to travel abroad, thus no reason to have a passport. Unfortunately, for many in the US, global geographical knowledge is limited.

While discussing using proper terms and references, the travel team should use the correct technical terms when interacting with the client. A client once told me that suppliers presenting to his company often used incorrect technical terms common to the industry that anyone knowledgeable of the industry would know and use. He said that contractors who do not use the proper technical phrases and words when speaking to client subject matter experts are often considered insufficiently familiar with the industry to provide the services needed.

Cultural Immersion

Your first visit to a country typically generates a desire to dive further into the culture via foods, books, language and movies. If you are like me, a country or a city on a map is just a spot on a piece of paper; it is faceless, intangible and has little meaning. The map comes alive after visiting the country and projects an entirely different feeling of familiarity, memories and natural sense. It is like going on a safari in Africa. When you return home, the wildlife shows you see on TV have a completely different meaning and interest level. Like me, a map does not mean much until you have traveled over it. International

travel and cultural immersion ignite interests that might otherwise lie dormant.

Conform to Cultural Mannerisms

Various typical mannerisms in your home country may be offensive, rude, or just bad manners in the countries you travel to. You must be aware of inappropriate or offensive mannerisms for each country, as presented in the book *Kiss, Bow, or Shake Hands*. We all know not to use the thumbs up or OK hand sign in certain countries. The safest policy is not to use any hand signs. In the Middle East and many parts of India and Africa, people typically use their right hand for eating, greeting, and touching. Some consider the left hand unclean, so in these countries, you should never use this hand for anything publicly. Several cultures consider crossing your legs to be rude. Blowing one's nose in front of others is certainly not good manners anywhere. If it is necessary to blow your nose, step away or out of the room before doing so. In the Middle East, do not show the bottom of your shoes. In parts of Asia, nodding your head means a disagreement, while shaking your head left to right means agreement.

The main point is to research what mannerisms are acceptable and unacceptable in each country we travel to, then conform. Doing so will communicate to your client host that you are culturally aware, adaptable and your company is a potential business partner.

Political Questions

Your personal political or religious views must not become an issue with the client. Discussing the host country or your home country's political, religious, or geopolitical matters should be avoided entirely. However, based on the same state of readiness theory as an elevator pitch, you should have an immediate prepared response if asked about your home country's political situation. Such questions are expected,

especially near election times. One neutral response might be something like: "That is a great question. The political situation in my country is quite complex, and it will be interesting to see how it all plays out." Always be prepared.

Loose Lips Sink Ships

Never make a derogatory comment about the meeting or the client, assuming that you are alone, for example, in restrooms, at a bar, or in a restaurant. Never think that others in your space (wherever you may be) do not speak English, including drivers. I know of a situation where, during a meeting break, colleagues went into the client's restroom, and one team member made derogatory comments about the client and the meeting. Then to their great surprise, a client meeting attendee, having heard the negative comments, stepped out from a bathroom stall. The situation with the client was bad enough before this happened. Always be discreet and careful of what, where, and when you make any negative or derogatory comments. It is best not to say anything negative unless you are in a safe location to do so. If you think you are being overheard, say something complimentary about the client, the city, or similar.

Another situation was in a client meeting. A colleague in his home language made a culturally derogatory comment about one of the attendees, thinking that the attendee would not understand. After the meeting, the attendee came forward and spoke fluently in the same foreign language, saying, "My grandmother was from country X. She and I communicated regularly in language X." Stories like these make chills run up one's spine. All the arduous work, time and cost invested in developing client relationships and the trip can immediately go up in smoke because a colleague makes a single senseless and derogatory statement about the client or the business, even if the comment is intended to be a harmless joke. I have heard of several instances where an English speaker who was fluent in the language used by his

colleagues did not reveal his fluency until months after hearing the other's discussions about him. Loose lips can destroy an otherwise successful business development trip or relationships with a colleague.

Sharing Culture at the Dinner Table

My experience is that the best venue for establishing business working relationships is over a meal, especially with other cultures. Sharing a leisurely meal can be an international ice breaker. James A. Michener said it well, "If you reject the food, ignore the customs, fear the religion and avoid the people, you might better stay home."

Your client may suggest a local restaurant with cuisine typical in their country. Eating and enjoying the local food, drink and music with your host is a bonding experience. Unfortunately, the opposite is also true. At client dinners, I have seen colleagues who openly disliked the local food and ordered something more in line with what they eat at home. Assume that you or a colleague have a problem with the local cuisine. In that case, it might be best not to attend the meal, but not participating will not advance the relationship and may be taken as a sign of disrespect, confirming the client's perception of the stereotype 'Ugly American' or other common negative nationality references. To successfully work internationally with diverse cultures, you must immerse yourself in that culture through the local cuisine, national drink and music. Let your client know that you genuinely enjoy sharing the cultural experience. I visualize the client thinking, "If this person cannot eat and drink with his potential business partner, how can we work together?" Your participation and genuine enjoyment in the meal is a social icebreaker and goes a long way in strengthening the business and personal relationship.

While having drinks in Mexico at a popular cantina with a potential joint venture partner, a music video of a famous Mexican singer was

projected onto a large screen. The Mexicans immediately turned their full attention to the performance. One of my colleagues loudly and very sarcastically asked, "Who is that guy?" only to learn it was Luis Miguel, whose love songs were responsible for most of Mexico's relationships in those years, and many today. This same colleague declined my wife's offer of a California wine at our home and openly announced he did not drink American wine. Some people are not culturally suited for international business development responsibilities regardless of their technical capabilities.

A friend tells the story of an American company owner who instructed his sales team, preparing to travel to Greece and Italy to meet with clients, not to include the cost of any liquor consumed at client meals on their expense reports. My friend explained that it would be inhospitable and offensive (probably impossible) to host a client dinner in Southern Europe and not offer alcoholic beverages. The company owner had little understanding of these cultures and his customers. Interestingly, I have a friend who swears that most of his networking, and more importantly, business deals, were done over a nice dinner or at the bar.

Language

How you communicate with clients whose primary language is not English often demonstrates your ability to process cultural differences and put the client at ease. Your client may not speak perfect English, but your communication should not be, in any way, condescending. Your communication tone, rhythm, volume and general delivery should not differ from how you usually communicate with others. Fortunately for the English-speaking businessperson, most host country clients speak English fluently, especially the younger generations. The client's English language capabilities can be unfortunate for the English speaker, who often develops an ingrained

attitude that it is unnecessary to learn other languages since most clients speak excellent English.

Many of my former colleagues were from the Netherlands and were global travelers. The Dutch language is not widely spoken outside of the Netherlands. Contrary to English speakers, the Dutch person's assumption is: "I must learn other languages to work and communicate with my clients who certainly do not speak Dutch." My experience is that the Dutch can focus on a foreign language, study it diligently, and quickly use the language well, many fluently. The need to learn a second language governs the ability and speed to learn. The opposite situation for English speakers is regrettable. Most English speakers do not attempt to learn their client's language basics because they see no real need to learn. Host country clients who speak English appreciate your ability to greet them in the local language and know basic courtesy phrases such as 'thank you, please and you are welcome.' Clients appreciate you making any effort to learn the basics of their language and they usually quickly and respectfully switch back to English because they want to practice their English.

If your business requires frequent travel to a particular area of the world, you must invest in learning the language, even if your host speaks perfect English. You will achieve a much higher level of client respect by demonstrating a willingness to study and speak their language, even if you make grammatical errors, which you will. You will also gain a much better understanding and appreciation of the culture. I study Spanish and speak the language at an intermediate level, allowing me to travel comfortably in Spanish-speaking countries. However, I am not fluent and cannot fully understand all the discussions in an all-Spanish meeting. Nevertheless, I have survived Spanish language meetings (alone), where I did my best, with the client speaking slowly and using the most familiar words.

Ideally, at least one travel team member should be fluent in the client's language. This capability is especially true when meeting with

the client's operational personnel who typically will not speak English. Presentations delivered in the local language are always effective client relationship development tools. It is also important to inform the client if you have employees in your home office who are fluent in their language and can communicate with client personnel as required.

Host Country History

Geography shapes history and history shapes a country's culture. Therefore, preparation for international business development campaigns should include a reasonable understanding of the country's history. Such knowledge will contribute to understanding your client and the environment that constrains him.

To prepare for an important meeting with a Cuban American, I read *Fidel - A Critical Portrait* (Szulc, 1986). Before discussing the business, I told my client that I was most interested in knowing more about his life in Cuba, stating that I had recently read the book about Castro. He was pleased that I was curious and immediately started talking about his life in Cuba, explaining how his family left the country in the early 1960s after Castro's revolutionary government had expropriated their family's shipping company. Our first meeting focused on his early life experiences in Cuba, and we never broached the business item.

In our second meeting, also before discussing any business matters, my client gave me a photo of his 1944-45 high school graduating class at the Jesuit-run prep school, El Colegio de Belén, which was one of the two great preparatory boys' schools in Havana (the other being La Salle). From the class of 40 boys, my client first pointed to his photo and then to Fidel Castro's picture. He and Castro were classmates, lived in the same dorm for four years and were teammates on the school's baseball team. The personal connection we

established by discussing his life experiences in Cuba unquestionably facilitated the business relationship. My sincere interest in knowing more about Cuba and listening to my client talk about his life experiences made the business relationship enjoyable – and the business outcome was extraordinarily positive.

Cultural Connectors

My experience is that international clients value connections between their country, culture and you. I continue to be amazed by the positive change in Latin American clients' attitudes towards me (and, by extension, my employer) once they learn that my wife is Latin American. Any direct or indirect international or cultural connection you can link with your international client is important to developing the business relationship. These links might include friends and colleagues from your client's country that you might invite to casual dinners or other social affairs with your client. Cultural connectors are incredible business development tools.

Multiple Trip Requirement for Relationship Development

Successful international business relationships are developed naturally over time and through regular and well-timed follow-up trips, meetings, lunches and dinners. The personal connection is key to all international business dealings, especially in Latin countries. I have worked for managers who did not understand this and expected immediate commercial results in these countries. They believed that a single complex business development campaign to Latin countries should immediately generate at least one business opportunity.

A client compliment that has always meant very much to me was my 'atypical' approach to business development. In many countries, relationship development always precedes business discussions.

Some cultures are perceived as being all business-focused with minimal investment in personal relationships. Much of my business is in Latin America and I have learned the value of first developing the relationship. Perhaps trying to be a bit more atypical in our approach to international business and relationships is a worthy goal.

Host Country Key Information

Take the time to learn host country facts and data before traveling. Learn the names of the host country's president, prime minister, and the CEO of the larger client companies you will visit. We assume everyone knows our country's president's or prime minister's name (for good or bad), but many people do not take the time, or demonstrate respect, to learn the host country's key data. The worst thing that can happen is that the client mentions their prime minister or president's name in a discussion and someone on the travel team asks, "Who is this is Mr. X you refer to?" Unfortunately, I have seen this happen. Put yourself in your client's shoes relative to what host country information they expect you to know. Alternatively, what level of knowledge would you expect your client to have when visiting your country?

Importance of Simple Cultural Experiences

One of my favorite activities is to patronize the same street-side shoeshine 'bolero' when visiting Mexico City. The best shoeshine and certainly the most enjoyable in the world may be in Mexico City. The professional boleros are unionized, have health insurance programs and other fantastic membership benefits. These professionals have an unbelievably effective local network. After several shines, you have a new friend who will always be at that exact spot Monday through Friday, like clockwork. Get to know his name because he is a fantastic information resource for anything you need on the streets. I have taken an extra suitcase full of shoes to my professional bolero, Juan

Carlos, to shine the week I am in Mexico City. For one trip, he knew I had a flight home that Friday afternoon. He was busy, running late and my shoes were not ready. The next thing I knew, his wife and three children arrived to assist and ensure that the shoes were nicely shined, wrapped in newspapers, packed and ready for me to take home. I take the time to share this simple cultural activity, which I also share with my Mexico City clients, who fully appreciate and understand the experience. Take advantage of simple cultural experiences while traveling and you will have a much better understanding and appreciation of the culture of countries you travel to.

Taking a Local Approach

Taking a different local culture approach to business might produce the best results and be very enjoyable. A European friend was invited to represent his company on the board of directors of one of the company's joint ventures in Spain. Before his appointment to the board, his company was represented by executives who would fly into Madrid the morning of the meeting and then fly out immediately afterward. As the new board member representing his company's interests, my friend took the local approach. He flew into Madrid early the day before the meeting and returned home a day or two after the meeting. With this schedule, he attended the informal pre-meeting dinner with the other board members. He also participated in a long afternoon Spanish lunch on the day after the board meeting, typically including local wines and cigars. His comment regarding the pre-board meeting was, "Now we had the real meeting. The dinner the night before the formal meeting was where all the important decisions were made. The purpose of the formal board meeting the next day was to confirm the decisions informally agreed to the night before at the dinner!"

The above story is an excellent example of what can be missed by not adapting to, and participating in, the local business customs. The

previous foreign board members had not spent the time required to develop more personal and meaningful relationships with the Spanish board members, as did my friend. The Spaniards commented that they had never had a better relationship with his company. My friend has a wealth of stories like this. One common thread in his stories is his ability to understand and mix effectively with other cultures – all supported by his incredible networking skills.

Over my career, I have observed executives who wanted others to see them as ultra-efficient in their time management. They would brag about flying in and out of a country for a client meeting the same day, sleeping on the return flight home and back in their office the following morning. Without a doubt, they were efficient using only one day away from the office and cost-efficient by sleeping on the plane instead of a hotel. However, as illustrated in the story above, they lost valuable opportunities to develop a closer cultural working relationship with the client through dinners and other opportunities to grow the relationship. In international business, you must invest in the time required to interact with the client in their own culture.

No Politics or Jokes

When traveling globally and working with other cultures, refrain from telling jokes or joking in general. Something funny to one culture may be offensive to another. You will typically communicate with your client in English, which may not be their first language. Their interpretation of the joke might be understood entirely differently from what you intend. I have always heard that a person is truly proficient in a second language when one can tell a joke in that language. My experience is not to joke with anyone in any language who is not a close friend. Making comments intended as a joke can backfire in any relationship, especially with other cultures. For lighter communications with your foreign hosts over dinner and drinks, the best advice is to discuss travel, sports, family and hobbies.

Political polarization is exceptionally high in the US and worldwide today, even within families. As international travelers, we must listen and understand where others are coming from as we network and develop projects. Also, we must be extra sensitive to the feelings of those who have political, religious, environmental and social views different from our own. Our goal must be to learn from those we interact with, not express our personal beliefs.

Conform

We must conform to the host country's culture, blend in, and not stick out. We all have seen situations in a restaurant or bar where expatriates gather in a group and communicate in a loud or boisterous manner. Everyone in the restaurant or bar becomes annoyed and can hear their comments. If everyone in the place behaves in this manner, it may be more acceptable. The point is not to stand out in any conduct that does not conform to the host country. We always want to be culturally normal and blend in. Think global and act local.

Where are you from?

This discussion may seem trivial to some readers. I always feel it helps to know the home country of the person I am speaking with. Some people are offended when asked the direct question, "Where are you from?" I have seen people turn and walk away from a conversation when asked this direct question. I am always curious about one's country of origin because I want to connect with them, especially if I have traveled to their home country. My experience is that knowing something about a person's home country is a quick connector and encourages communication. It can break the ice. The question is, how to courteously ask a person their nationality without appearing to be a nosy person. One option is to ask if they are from the city that you are physically in at the time. In this scenario, they

have the option of answering as they feel appropriate. For example, they might say, "Yes, I have lived here in Bogota for 15 years, but I was born in Spain." Never assume that a person is from a particular country because of their appearance, then ask if your assumption is correct. Most people are offended, especially when they are not from the country you assumed. Always keep assumptions to yourself. Typically, after talking with the person for a brief period, their country of origin will usually be revealed.

Cultural Training

There are numerous opportunities in your home country to become more familiar with the culture of the country you will be visiting, principally through restaurants, food markets, books, movies and host country nationals living in your home country. Spending time with these resources is productive when preparing for your first trip to a country. For example, if traveling to Asia, have dinner at an authentic Asian restaurant where the clientele is Asian. You will know that the restaurant serves authentic Asian food if it is full of people of Asian descent. Study the menu, identify traditional food selections you like, use chopsticks, drink the tea and immerse yourself in the culture. Best of all, invite your Asian friend to the dinner and have them instruct you in local table etiquette and customs such as tapping your right hand on the table near your teacup, meaning "thank you" after others refill it. Your client will appreciate your basic familiarity with the local foods, table manners, customs, and proper use of chopsticks and other tableware. Pre-trip experiences will enhance your confidence level and you will be much more comfortable and enjoy sharing the meal with your international hosts.

You should know which local customs your client does not expect you to conform to. Trying to act local when not trained in the tradition is not advisable. One example may be using your right-hand fingers instead of a fork to eat certain problematic foods. You do not want to

look foolish in attempting to be local. It may be best to eat in a manner you are comfortable with and accustomed to. The web is an excellent source of information to prepare you for proper international table etiquette.

Corruption

Working internationally, you will be exposed to corruption at some point in your career, often associated with large contracts. A contract award may be contingent upon your company working through a particular local agent or a specific local partner. If the local agent or partner bribes client personnel to be awarded the contract, your unawareness of the corruption does not absolve you. I am aware of companies who used local agents to manage the kickbacks to the client, such payments made by the agent from their higher than standard commissions. Frequently, corruption involves national governmental officials. For Americans, a violation of the Foreign Corrupt Practices Act usually takes the form of a bribe, either directly or indirectly (i.e., through agents), paid by a US business to a foreign official to influence an award of business or to gain an unfair advantage in business dealings. As discussed in Chapter 2, protecting your reputation is paramount to your career success, and we must not be involved in business relationships that depend on corrupt practices. If you become aware of these situations, immediately request to be removed from the account relationship.

Part 3
Project Tender Responsibilities and Future Challenges

CHAPTER 12

The Business Development Manager's Responsibilities for the Tender Process and Contract Handover

FIRST, SOME TERMINOLOGY: THE tender process, commonly known in the US as the bidding process, is defined as "the process in which the client invites a select group of suppliers to submit a formal proposal for a product, a service, or a construction project." Both terms are acceptable, but 'tender' is more common internationally.

You probably do not have tender management experience if you are new to the profession. Managing, preparing and delivering a complex proposal is always challenging. The guidance provided in this

chapter provides general guidance for managing the tender process. For the student, the information shared will set you apart from others when interviewing for international positions.

The Tender (Bidding) Process

The tender process is exceptionally time-sensitive and the time allowed to deliver the proposal to the client never seems enough. The ultimate goal of the business development process is that your company is awarded a profitable contract. To accomplish this, your team may have invested years developing the client relationship and influencing the tender requirements to match your company's capabilities.

Managing a tender, preparing and submitting the proposal is often the responsibility of the business development or commercial manager. You will have the longest direct exposure to the client, the highest level of project knowledge, and the best understanding of the client's needs and expectations for the tender deliverables. The skillsets you rely on for the tender process are related to, but different from, those employed while developing the client relationship. Your versatility and ability to switch gears throughout the business development cycle are vital to your career's success.

The tender process is, as they say, "where the rubber meets the road." Typically, only a select group of prequalified suppliers are invited to participate in large tenders. The number of participants invited to submit bids is limited because each proposal requires considerable client evaluation time. Structuring the proposal to highlight your company's differentiators is invaluable and best presented using a techno-commercial overview at the start of the tender document that demonstrates why your proposal is the best option for the client. The client will use a well-written proposal summary as a guide, or benchmark, to review other bidders'

proposals. Some bidders may intentionally omit items from their proposal, with the intent that these items later become expensive variation orders. This approach is a sure way to be disqualified early on in the process. All proposal requirements must be brought to the fore at the tender time to ensure that all bids are scored based on the same criteria. All information requested in the client's request for proposal must be considered and addressed in your bid.

Tender Team and Focus

A robust international tender team will include a multi-disciplined group of colleagues with expertise in the areas: commercial, operational, technical, Safety, Health, Environment and Quality (SHE-Q), financial, legal, and governmental affairs. Each team member should clearly understand the deliverables relative to the client's needs and expectations. The focus should be on the substance of the tender package and not generating a large volume of material. An impressively thick and attractively bound proposal document, full of verbal presentation, corporate brochures and other publications that does not concisely focus on client deliverable expectations may not be considered by the client. Boilerplate corporate information should be appropriately segregated in the tender documents to not dilute the core information specific to the proposal. A well-written executive summary should accompany all tender submissions.

The following is an overview of the tender process and outlines the business development manager's specific responsibilities for proposal team management, bid preparation and delivery:

Components of the Tender Process

1.   *Registration in Client Approved Vendor System*

Typically, registration in the client's approved vendor system requires submitting documentation supporting your company's ownership, technical capabilities, project experience, safety record and financial strength. If your company's safety record is not in line with industry standards, your application may be rejected. Anti-bribery and anti-corruption policies and procedures are closely reviewed in the supplier registration processes.

It is important to note that most clients will allow you to register as an approved vendor outside of a formal tender process. It is always beneficial to register in the client's purchasing system before a formal tender is opened because pre-registered suppliers may be the first companies clients invite to tender.

2. *Client Selection of Companies to Tender – Invitation to Tender*

The client evaluates companies capable of offering the required services then invites a select group to bid. Companies selected are sent formal invitations to tender to which they must promptly respond and inform the client of their intention to participate or decline participation.

3. *Tender Resources*

Large and complex tenders require a significant commitment of financial and human resources. The cost to prepare and assemble a large and complex proposal can easily range between $500,000 to $1,000,000. Management must be made aware of pending tenders as soon as possible to ensure that adequate human and financial resources are available to prepare and deliver the proposal on time.

4.   Request for Proposal (RFP) Sent to Bidders

The RFP is the client's mechanism for inviting a group of potential suppliers to respond to their needs. The documents are typically delivered by express mail or via a website dedicated to the tender process, as hard copies are usually voluminous. The RFP package generally is divided into the following sections:

1.   Technical;
2.   Commercial; and
3.   Contractual (terms and conditions).

The RFP will include the rules of the tender process, important dates, including document clarifications, submission deadline, bid award target date, contract start date and other date-specific information.

The client will request that you acknowledge the receipt of the RFP documents by completing an acknowledgment form confirming receipt, your understanding of the tender requirements, and your intent to bid or decline participation. The acknowledgment should be completed and promptly returned to the client to demonstrate an elevated level of interest in participating in the tender. Waiting to submit the acknowledgment on the due date may communicate a reduced level of interest to the client.

5.   Technical Proposal

The technical and commercial proposals are submitted in separate sealed envelopes. Theoretically, the client first evaluates the technical proposal without being biased by the commercial proposal. If the supplier's technical proposal is accepted, then the commercial proposal will be considered.

The tender team's goal is to present an optimally priced technical solution that is in complete compliance with the client's RFP deliverability requirements and sets your proposal apart from the competitors, allowing the client to compare your submission to the stated deliverable requirements efficiently. You should know your competitors well enough to anticipate their technical and commercial proposals, then develop a superior solution that is also commercially viable. Invest time in determining how your competitors will present their proposal.

It is very useful to understand the client's primary reasons for the project, such as improving cash flow, enhancing operator safety or obtaining innovative technology. Once the client's needs are fully understood, repeatedly present throughout the tender documents and in different terms, how your proposal explicitly meets the client's needs. It is important to remember that tendering is not merely a process of responding directly to the RFP but also establishing your company's ability to satisfy the client's needs

Often the client's RFP documents do not adequately reflect their project needs and expectations, and these areas must be identified and clarified with the client. Success is dependent on your ability to evaluate how your proposed solutions to the client's needs best fit into their existing organization and infrastructure versus offering solutions that are more focused on your company's resources. Winning solutions will be highly focused on the client.

There may be opportunities to provide the client a second side proposal for additional services that encompass a broader scope of work that you become aware of during the tender process that further supports the client's needs.

6. Commercial Proposal - Request for Quotation (RFQ)

The RFQ requests a monetary proposal. It is a legally binding document in which you propose contract pricing, warranties, schedules and other commercial details of your bid. An enlightened client will award the contract to the best value, not the lowest price, and a financially constrained client will award the lowest price. If your proposal offers the client the best value, this should be highlighted throughout the proposal, as the client will be paying for this extra value versus the lowest cost option.

In your response to the RFQ, you must consider that the client already has a budget prepared, reflecting the existing market, technology and operational conditions. Your quotation should be prepared along the same lines. If you bid too low, the client will be given the impression that you will use inappropriate materials and cut corners. If you bid too high, the client will think that you are out to gouge them. Preparing the winning quotation is highly dependent on understanding the market and your client's operating philosophies.

It is important to understand that budgetary pressures may conflict with the client organization's optimum operational solution. Try to determine the client's internal politics of the project and use the knowledge to your advantage in your proposal.

7. Contract Terms and Conditions (T&Cs)

A company will often present a winning technical and commercial proposal; however, the parties cannot agree on contract terms and conditions, typically the liability limitation clauses. Many clients will add a third section to the tender to minimize the time required to negotiate contract terms and conditions. In this section, the bidder either accepts the client's

terms and conditions or proposes modified terms and conditions that may or may not be negotiated.

Liability clauses often are not mutually agreed and the bidder with the second-best technical and commercial proposal, who accepts the client requested liability limitations, is awarded the contract. Unfortunately for the client, contractors who accept the higher liability limitations may not be the most financially capable company bidding, yet accepting the higher liability limits. This phase of the tendering process is always difficult for both the client and the contractor.

8.   Tender Award

The contract is awarded to the bidder who has offered the client the best combined technical and commercial solutions and can negotiate mutually acceptable contract terms and conditions. Therefore, your company's lowest price proposal may not be awarded the contract if your submission has not differentiated your company from the competition nor clearly demonstrated your capabilities to meet the client's needs.

9.   Contract Start-Up and Handover

After the contract is awarded and signed, the business development manager will hand over primary client relationship responsibilities to your company's operations group or contract manager. Still, the business development manager should continue the broader client relationship as future business opportunities are usually generated from a successful first-client relationship.

Corporate Structures for Managing the Tender Process

Companies use different organizational structures for tender preparation. Large project-oriented companies will have a dedicated tender department that prepares multiple complex and large dollar value proposals each year. Smaller companies will typically prepare a limited number of proposals annually using an ad-hoc tender team comprised of knowledgeable employees from commercial, technical, financial and legal departments. The person-hour requirements for preparing and delivering a large tender can be enormous. In smaller companies, employees are often stressed because tender preparation time requirements are on top of their day-to-day responsibilities.

The Business Development Manager's Responsibilities for the Tender

Your tender responsibilities will depend on your company's size and whether or not it has a dedicated tender department. In all scenarios, the business development manager should fulfill the following roles and responsibilities:

1. *Continued Client Point Person or Tender Team Manager*

    As the business development manager, you should assume primary responsibility for the overall tender process and continue as the client's point person. Even if your company has a formal tender department, you should continue as the primary interface with the client. Under no circumstances should the tender be prepared and submitted without your input relative to your knowledge and understanding of client expectations.

    Regardless of the level of your responsibilities for preparing the tender, you must be thoroughly familiar with the tender

documents and closely monitor all submission due dates. You should be copied on all tender team emails, monitor tender team progress and intervene as soon as you see any issues that might impair the quality or delay the timely delivery of the proposal. Once you become aware that the tender submission date may not be met, you should formally communicate with the client the reasons for the delay and request that the tender submission date be extended. It is important to remember that the client views you as their point person in the relationship and considers you responsible for the proposal process.

2. *Delivery of Proposal Documents to the Client*

Where possible, the business development manager should hand-deliver the proposal to the client and receive written confirmation of receipt of documents stating the time, date of receipt and signed by the client representative receiving the documents. If delivery is electronic, request electronic delivery and confirmation receipts; then send a separate email to the client requesting confirmation of timely delivery and receipt of your proposal. You certainly do not want to be disqualified because the documents were delivered to the client's office as required but not delivered to the appropriate person, internally, on time.

3. *Formal Tender Presentation to Client*

As a finalist in a tender process, being asked by the client to formally present your proposal in person is an excellent opportunity to highlight areas in which your proposal exceeds the competition. You should assume overall responsibility for preparing the presentation; however, it is most effective if the tender team members who prepared each section of the proposal presents their respective area (commercial, technical and legal). (See Chapter 9 for client presentations discussion).

Presentations should be focused, concise and in full accordance with the client's guidelines, including time limits. The tender team should develop a detailed list of potential questions that might be asked by the client and prepare a scripted response. Any time overruns should be due to client questions and interest in your proposal, not the result of your poorly organized presentation.

Your team should prepare for tender presentation meetings as attorneys would using a mock trial, utilizing technically knowledgeable colleagues as role players to test an array of responses to client questions. Closely monitor the client's body language during the meeting. A former colleague tells me that women with children are most proficient in reading body language. This team member can be of significant value in contract negotiations. A third team member should prepare minutes as the meeting progresses and present them to the client for review and approval at the end of the session.

4.   Project Handover

Handover of the awarded contract to the contract manager, operations manager, or other group responsible for managing the contract should be well-planned and seamless. Project handover overlap is extremely important to the client. Therefore, the tender manager should monitor the process and use any soft power with management and operations to influence a proper and smooth handover.

5.   *Continued Client Involvement*

The business development manager's continued liaison with the client after contract handover and project start-up will facilitate new project opportunities.

Ad-Hoc Tender Preparation Guidelines

The following list outlines the tender manager's general responsibilities when the tender team is comprised of employees from various departments (i.e., an ad-hoc team – not a formal corporate tender department):

a. Management designates a tender manager (ideally the business development manager).

b. The tender manager prepares a detailed schedule of information requested by the RFP, then sets the dates information must be completed and submitted to him/her for review. (To facilitate client review of the proposal, all proposal information and schedules submitted should mirror the client RFP numbering and referencing system. The goal is to make the proposal documents easy for the client to follow.)

c. The tender manager prepares a tender team organization chart, proposes team members, and requests management approval.

d. Management formally communicates the team's organization to the tender team members and the appropriate corporate departments, requesting full cooperation and support for the project.

e. The tender manager communicates team member responsibilities and agrees on the required completion dates for each item in the RFP.

f. The tender manager maintains regular contact with each tender team member and prepares a weekly progress report distributed to all team members and management. Periodic virtual team meetings must be well-organized following a meeting agenda.

g. Tender preparation areas that typically require the most extensive time investment (and potentially delaying proposal preparation) include: contract pricing calculations, contract legal reviews, technical design and the preparation of various plans required by the RFP (operations, risk assessments, SHE-Q, training, etc.). The tender manager must closely monitor progress in these areas.

h. If possible, the tender team should prepare the proposal in person, working shoulder-to-shoulder. If this is not an option, the tender manager and a select group of team members should sit together at the end of the process to finalize the preparation and assembly of the proposal. The proposal should be completed at least one week before the tender submission due date.

Fundamental to the proposal preparation process is the opportunity for the tender team to work together face-to-face. Working in person allows exchanging ideas, communicating and interacting in ways not possible working remotely. Proposal quality is highly dependent on the team working together in person.

Summary

When reviewing the business development manager's responsibilities for the tender process, one might ask how you can simultaneously manage the tender process and continue the ongoing business development activities with other clients and projects? For a smaller company, winning one major contract may be so financially important that the company will temporarily cease business development activities and focus all company resources on the one project being tendered. Normal business development activities resume after the tender is submitted.

In closing this chapter, I want to highlight the broad range of your responsibilities as the business development manager throughout the project development cycle. Your responsibility is not merely a function of identifying potential client projects, 'door opening', introductory meetings and client entertaining, then moving on to the next potential client. Instead, today's business development manager is a versatile and highly trained professional who is entrepreneurial by nature, understands the client's drivers, and carries a broad base of capabilities and skills in their toolbox to manage multiple responsibilities throughout the business development cycle.

CHAPTER 13

Post-Pandemic Inspired Challenges, Organization and Opportunities

THE PANDEMIC OF 2020-22 was an event that changed how we network, plan and execute international business development projects and campaigns. Many of the changes will be permanent; mainly, more people working permanently from home, working in hybrid office arrangements, reduced international travel requirements and increased reliance on virtual communications. Unforeseen life-changing random events will continue to occur, be they wars, economic meltdowns, plagues and events yet to be named or classified. Virtually overnight, a completely unforeseen event can obliterate a seeming state of quasi-normalcy. The insightful business development professional will approach these situations with the

attitude of 'never let a crisis go to waste' and benefit by negotiating around and through the obstacles, thinking and acting outside the box.

Accelerated Change

Rapid changes in the way we conduct business were at various stages of progress before the pandemic. Technology has allowed previously disadvantaged groups globally to compete on a more even playing field in technology, engineering and business in general. For example, many of us did not have regular access to in-office IT assistance for our computer issues during the pandemic. The Microsoft technicians who remotely and efficiently managed my computer issues were based in India, the Philippines, or Central America. The quality of support was usually superb. One technical support call that best illustrated change to me was with a Filipina technician, I assume at daybreak in the Philippines, as I heard a rooster crowing loudly. It sounded like the rooster was sharing the microphone with the technician. I asked if there was a rooster in the room and the young technician very casually said, "Yes, right here on the window ledge." She confidently continued in control of my computer to resolve the issue. The rooster experience powerfully echoed the current trend of change. Like the Filipina, well-trained and competent technicians work remotely worldwide. Reliable technical support is now provided 24/7 from any part of the world with training, English language skills, electrical power, a computer and a WiFi connection. The Filipina technician's employment cost, I am sure, is a fraction of one working from San Francisco, Austin, or New York. The global playing field is being leveled quickly in all professions.

So how does this discussion relate to the position of international business development manager? First, it highlights the need for the business development professional to be proficient in using web-based technology to network, plan and execute business development

campaigns. Many business development professionals previously relied on face-to-face meetings using charisma-based strengths that will be less useful in the future because the business development process will depend more on virtual communications. Of course, personal face-to-face client interactions are always more effective, but the value of virtual communication and presentation skills are suddenly propelled in relative importance.

We can speculate and make assumptions about how we will work in the future. Still, without a doubt, personal face-to-face client contact will be reduced and, for many projects, will be pushed towards the end of the project development cycle. The business development manager, who relied heavily on personal charisma, must develop an 'E-Charisma'.

Virtual Travel is Cost-Effective

International travel is expensive and time-consuming, and virtual meetings are incredibly cost-effective and time-efficient. We can effectively cover a large swath of the globe from our home office in a few hours. A self-starting, well-organized, and digitally savvy professional can effectively generate an equivalent work output of multiple less-digitally skilled persons. Importantly, digital technology provides persons who cannot travel because of physical impairments an equal opportunity to achieve the same results as an unimpaired person. I am familiar with several situations in my business where the employees are physically challenged to travel. Still, working virtually, their performance in some cases significantly exceeds those who are not impaired and who have depended more on international travel, face-to-face meetings, client dinners and their charisma. An interesting exercise is to prepare a list of your normal daily activities, then circle those that absolutely cannot be performed virtually from your home office. This exercise was eye-opening and confirmed that the only missing link is travel and person-to-person contact.

One example of the efficient use of digital technology is for international bidding processes that require bidders to travel long distances to physically attend project site visits to better understand the client's requirements for the project. Project site visit trips can easily consume a minimum of three days and typically more, depending on project location and travel time. A colleague recently attended a project site visit in Central America using drone technology, virtually from his home office in California. The site visit was attended by multiple contractors from their home offices around the world. My colleague explained that the live drone video flyover of the project site was more effective than if he had traveled to the site. For example, participants could request the drone pilot to focus on specific site locations of interest to the contractors. Travel costs were zero and the total time incurred was two hours. The negative aspect was the irreplaceable benefits of person-to-person contact with the client. As previously stated, person-to-person client contact is the most compelling element of relationship development. Still, much of it will be moved closer to the end of the project development cycle for many projects.

How Will the Pandemic Affect International Business Travel?

The pandemic has complicated international travel, affecting how we build and maintain networks and plan and execute global market development campaigns. Travel medical documentation requirements, now referred to by many as Travel Medical Passports, will continue to develop. Hopefully, there will be a reasonable level of required consistency for the countries you travel to. Consider the following:

1. *Traveler Medical Documentation Requirements*

Travel Medical Passports will be maintained electronically using platforms that minimize the risk of falsifying these documents. Medical documentation and proof of medical insurance coverage are now required travel items for many countries and these documents have equal status with the passport and visa. The greatest challenge is the inconsistency of travel medical document requirements between countries.

2. *Client Enforced Travel Restrictions*

Clients may restrict in-person visits of suppliers and contractors traveling from specific areas of the world and require virtual meetings. Clients may enforce their own international visitors' policies, including varying quarantine enforcement policies, making it more difficult for international business development trip planning and execution. Any quarantine requirement impacts travel costs and travel time budgets.

3. *Work Visa Enforcement*

Before the pandemic, many countries did not enforce established work visa requirements for sales and marketing representatives entering the country. Instead, businesspersons would enter the country by completing a tourist visa form. More countries may start enforcing work visa regulations because of unemployment concerns in their countries or the need for foreign currency from visa applicants.

4. *Pressure on Expatriate Employment*

In the post-pandemic economy, companies maintaining employees internationally may re-evaluate expatriate

employment and travel costs and rely on less costly nationals and more on virtual communications with clients.

5. Visa Application Process Time

Visa requirements for some countries may become more stringent due to medical testing, immunization documentation and proof of medical insurance coverage – all requiring additional time to process documents and increasing consulate workloads. This added delay must be budgeted into the planning process. Companies must consider how enhanced visa requirements will affect their performance on awarded contracts. For example, the company's ability to provide contractually required expatriate employees to support the contracted requirements will be much more challenging than before the pandemic.

6. Air Transportation Cost, Schedules and Logistics

Flight availability, direct flight options and flight frequency are severely affected by pandemics, principally flights to remote and developing parts of the world, where many of the more significant new international projects are found. It will be much more challenging to reach these destinations, all of which must be budgeted and considered in travel planning and itineraries.

Traveling in North Africa in November 2021, during the COVID epidemic, I was scheduled to fly from Cairo, Egypt, in transit through London, then to the US. I carried all the required QR vaccination codes and a less than a 24-hour old negative test result. However, when checking in in Cairo for the flight, three hours before departure, I first learned that London Heathrow in transit passengers were required to present a special code for flight check-in, seemingly unique to flights to the UK. Cairo airport WiFi was intermittent, and I could not complete the

extraordinarily long and detailed online form to receive the passcode. Other passengers and I missed the flight. I purchased a ticket on the first available flight out on another airline and departed Cairo 18 hours later. Had I arrived at the airport 5 hours before the flight, I would have learned of the unique requirement early enough to have secured the special code. During this trip, I realized that airline personnel were often confused about the COVID protocols of certain destination airports, as was the case with London Heathrow. During pandemics, you must double-check the protocols on the airline websites and check into your flight extra early to have sufficient time to recover from issues as I experienced in Cairo.

Virtual Meeting Execution

Thanks to the pandemic and necessity, we have become much more proficient in planning and conducting virtual meetings and digital collaboration skills have suddenly been propelled in importance Below is a summary of key points I have observed in the virtual meetings that I planned or attended during the pandemic.

1. The primary objective of an introductory client meeting is to introduce your company and team and develop the opportunity for a second meeting more focused on the client's project requirements and your company's ability to provide solutions. The optimum time limit for a virtual client introductory meeting is not more than 45 minutes, assuming that the meeting is well-planned and organized using an agenda.

2. Test the virtual meeting platform before the meeting. Ask the client host if their assistant or another person could assist in testing the equipment. I have attended too many virtual meetings where technical issues spoiled the meeting, such as inadequate bandwidth for the PowerPoint and other presentations.

3. Background surroundings should be simple and not distracting. Check fore and backlight levels. A daylit window behind you will hide your face in the darkness as the camera tries to cope. Too much light and your face will not look good. Adjust your camera so your head and shoulders occupy most of the screen. Consider using a corporate logo/green screen combination as background.

4. Watch other users in the meeting and emulate behavior and images that you find appealing.

5. When not speaking, mute your microphone and refrain from head nodding, neck straightening, etc. Motion catches the eye and detracts attention from the speaker.

6. Consider using an external camera on a stand rather than the camera on your laptop. It will provide more flexibility in framing the shot than using the laptop camera.

7. Several days before the virtual meeting, send client attendees a limited amount of introductory information such as brochures, a short letter of introduction and consider sending a copy of the presentation. In a 30-to-45-minute virtual meeting, there is not sufficient time to review and discuss all of these items.

8. Meetings must be highly organized to execute a successful virtual meeting within a limited time. Meetings must start on time, and time will pass quickly. All information to be shared on the virtual screen must be immediately available. Searching for the material on your computer will waste time, annoying the participants.

9. We must be agile in our virtual presentation. Clients may comment that they are familiar with your company and suggest that the meeting move to the primary agenda items. You must

then adjust your presentation and meeting plan accordingly. Know your material well and be flexible.

10. Regardless of the number of points to be discussed, you should always prepare a formal agenda which will be the primary map for the meeting. (See Tool No. 4 and 5). Preparing an agenda is vital even if there are only one or two items to discuss. Before the meeting, send the agenda to the client for their review and approval. Copy and paste the agenda to the note section of the electronic meeting invitations. Send all attendees another copy of the agenda on the morning of the meeting as a reminder. The agenda will typically include:

   a. Local meeting times for attendees in each time zone.
   b. A copy of the virtual meeting platform meeting link, meeting number and password.
   c. Attendees, with their company name, position, location and email address.
   d. Meeting objective(s).
   e. Agenda items should list the person's name responsible for leading the discussion.
   f. Links for PDF corporate items such as a brochure or Letter of Introduction.

11. To ensure that your team is sufficiently familiar with the client company, provide each colleague with client background information before the meeting.

12. If you plan to make a PowerPoint presentation, limit the slides to a few perfectly prepared slides. There is not enough time for many slides, and most importantly, virtual meetings will flow better if available time is used in open discussions. Three well-thought-out slides presenting your company are ideal if you can accomplish this feat. This is extremely difficult for most of us.

13. It is important to reiterate that the basic principles of virtual and in-person meetings are the same. The challenge is to achieve a similar result in a virtual meeting as in a person-to-person meeting.

14. After each meeting, send the client a brief thank you and a summary of any action items. Where appropriate, minutes should be promptly prepared and sent to the client for review and approval. I suggest sending the note of appreciation the day of the meeting, but no later than the next day.

In closing this chapter, working virtually, we should invest in the best technology available and maximize its value to override the obstacles we face in these more challenging times.

Part 4
International Business Travel

CHAPTER 14

In-Transit Challenges
and Hurdles - Land and
Air

IT IS SIMPLE. IF we do not arrive at the destination, we will not realize the trip's business goals. A simple travel mistake has the potential to end an international business trip. We cannot always rely on our common sense to control these threats - a minor error can cause significant problems. Mistakes made while traveling globally are not as forgiving and so easy to recover from as those made traveling domestically.

Basic Rules for Flight Connections

A basic rule of travel, which we all know too well but do not always follow, is to arrive at the airport for international flights at least three hours in advance in the US and as the airlines recommend in other countries, often more than three hours, especially during pandemic periods. Add at least one extra hour to the airline's requirement. I have flown from international airports where flights were closed out one hour before departure and it was impossible to check-in afterward. My experience traveling internationally during the COVID-19 pandemic was that extraordinarily early flight check-in was needed to deal with constantly changing COVID-19 documentation requirements. We all have missed flights because of misinformation, misjudgments, laxity, or events entirely outside our control. You have little control over delays in route to the airport, such as auto mechanical issues, traffic jams and accidents. When traveling internationally, it is not worth the extra hour of sleep, the Starbucks coffee stop, or any other activity that might interfere with a timely arrival at the airport. You will arrive at the airport much more relaxed and less likely to make simple, potentially devastating travel blunders when you budget extra transit time to the airport.

Before booking international flights, carefully review the preliminary flight plan and discuss any tight connections with your travel agent. A professional agent will know if connection times are reasonable considering the arrival and departure gates and terminal locations. Sufficient time must be budgeted for connections in countries where geopolitical risk is high. Departing and in-transit passengers often must pass through multiple security checkpoints, requiring thorough body and luggage searches.

In the early 1990s, security levels in Colombia were highly elevated. Before boarding any flight, passengers were meticulously searched at four different checkpoints, of which two were military police. On a recent trip to Egypt, security was exceptionally high,

passing through three security checkpoints. Travelers were advised to arrive at the airport three hours before the flight, which was insufficient, as I discussed in Chapter 13. A professional travel agent can access airport security information and determine if flight connection times are adequate.

In geopolitically difficult parts of the world, an excellent option is to utilize a certified agency (expediter) to meet you at your arrival gate, escort you through the security checkpoints, take care of all the paperwork and deliver you to the departure gate if in transit, or to your hotel if at the destination. The value of these services is well worth the added expense. To the extent possible, strive to book direct flights or flights not requiring a change of planes.

Before departing to the airport or while en route, you may receive an airline text message or email stating that your departure time is delayed. More than once, I have learned the hard way to never rely on these messages as being accurate, then delay your arrival at the airport. Planes either make up for the delay or the information is wrong.

When making international flight connections, regardless of the amount of spare time you think you have, after landing, go directly to the connecting flight departure gate. Verbally confirm the flight's status with the gate agent and reconfirm your seat assignment, even if you hold a boarding pass issued at the originating airport. When transferring to a connecting flight, you should not assume that the airport flight information boards are updated and are correct. Additionally, public address system announcements of gate and flight time changes are not always audibly clear foreign accents may be difficult to understand, or your hearing may be impaired. Also, never assume that the information on the boarding pass issued at the originating airport is correct or unchanged.

Once, in a rush, I misread the boarding pass's seat number as the gate number. This error was incredibly foolish, but with limited time and running late, you may be nervous and it is easy to make simple mistakes that jeopardize your ability to make the connecting flight. Fortunately, we usually recover from these mistakes without consequences. Still, we can minimize the risks and the resulting pressure if we follow the commonsense and straightforward procedures that we all know well but do not always follow because they are commonsense.

Once you have reconfirmed that everything is in order, now is the time to go to a nearby restaurant or do some shopping. Lastly, always synchronize your device's time with the local time on the airline flight board and set the alarm on your phone for the return time to the departure gate.

A Serious Need for Ground Support

In my earlier years of international travel, a colleague and I traveled from Angola to Equatorial Guinea, then to the UAE. We booked a series of flights on regional airlines to save time and money, but mostly to see other parts of Africa. When we arrived in the Congo, customs collected and soon returned in-transit passenger's passports, except for my colleague and me. We retrieved our passports after negotiating a final payment of $100. I was not feeling well and laid down on the dirt floor near the airline ticket counters, using my computer bag as a pillow. To give you an idea of how rustic the airport was, a giant rat ran directly at me while laying down, making a sharp turn to safety, centimeters short of my nose. A sight, in broad daylight, I will never forget.

My colleague then discovered that his airline ticket was missing from his bag. He was sure who had taken it and alerted a nearby police officer. The police officer motioned the thief and us into the men's

restroom, where he offered to retrieve the ticket from the thief for a fee of $100, of which $50 was for the police officer and $50 for the thief. We negotiated a total ticket repurchase payment of $50. Unfortunately, everyone wanted US Dollars and my colleague's Euros were of no use to us. We proceeded to the ticket counter to get the boarding pass for the next flight and the ticket agent asked to see the boarding pass stubs from our arriving flight, which I could not locate. The agent said the penalty for not having the arriving flight boarding pass receipt was $50. Fortunately, I found the receipt and avoided the penalty. (You should always maintain all flight documents received, including boarding passes). We walked to the local airline's tiny, hot and empty executive lounge and we each took a cold soft drink from the refrigerator, then took a well-needed short nap on the lounge couches. Our flight's boarding was announced and we started to leave the lounge only to be stopped at the door by the lady lounge manager, who said we owed $25 for the two soft drinks, usually complimentary in executive lounges. Considering all the fees we had already paid, we continued toward the boarding gate. The woman summoned a nearby police officer (a different police officer from the first one we dealt with), who demanded that we pay the $25 or miss our flight. My colleague's Euros were not accepted, so I negotiated $10 for the two soft drinks. The total fees paid were undoubtedly more than a professional expeditor would have cost.

My colleague and I were young and novice travelers and we had much more to learn about international travel. I remember him commenting that we should write a book about that trip. After more than 20 years, this is the result.

This story accentuates the importance of hiring an expeditor or agent support when traveling in complex and challenging parts of the world.

Flight Layover Lodging

Long international flights to remote parts of the world often require multiple flight changes and long-in-transit layovers, often overnight. For these layovers, you can either spend the night in an uncomfortable waiting lounge chair or go to a nearby hotel for a few hours' sleep and take a shower. Assuming that your airline is not arranging the layover hotel, I recommend staying at hotels at or near the airport. Otherwise, do not rely on a local cab driver's hotel suggestion, as their preference is seldom the safest and closest option. You are not familiar with the city, the morning traffic patterns or the local security issues, so it is best to stay as close to the airport as possible. The first wake-up option is your travel alarm, set to the correct local time zone, backed up by requests for a hotel wake-up call and a door knock wake up (best secured with a tip to the hotel desk clerk). You should never rely on a hotel wake-up call. You may not have access to your checked luggage for these layovers, so having a small bag of toiletries in your carry-on bag can be a lifesaver.

Airline Executive Lounges

A premier airline executive lounge membership is highly recommended for frequent international travelers. It is one of the few locations in developing world airports you can relax, have a snack or a light meal. In some lounges, you can shower and, if necessary, get some work done. Your luggage is typically secure in these lounges. Excessively long layovers and flight delays are much more tolerable when you can settle down in a clean and comfortable airport lounge. If your frequent flyer status does not provide the right to use these facilities, you can often pay an hourly use fee. Discuss the comprehensive benefits of purchasing a widely accepted airport executive lounge membership with your management.

Early Flight Boarding

If you are not flying business class, board the flight as early as possible to have sufficient overhead bin space to stow and maintain control over your carry-on luggage. If there is no bin space near your seat, you will have to use bins outside your direct sight. Once overhead space is filled, which frequently happens on the older aircraft flown in many parts of the world, you must gate-check the bags. Once checked, you have lost control over the items in those bags. In many international airports, items in checked baggage are highly subject to tampering and theft, as is the case in Venezuela, particularly well-known for things being taken from checked luggage.

In-Flight Use of Laptop Computers

Your laptop computer and mobile phone usually are the two tools you rely on most for an international business trip. These tools must be protected from damage and theft. I have had awful experiences using laptops while flying internationally. One instance was a domestic flight within Mexico on a small twin-engine aircraft. The flight was extremely turbulent and the flight attendant dropped a full can of soda on my laptop, shattering the screen.

In another incident, the gentlemen sitting next to me spilled a full glass of red wine onto my computer keyboard. I poured the wine out of the computer and it continued working. However, all the keys started sticking as the wine residue dried about an hour later. The laptop could not be repaired.

I lost another laptop, clearing a military security checkpoint in South America. With an automatic rifle strapped to his shoulder, a soldier examined the computer and dropped it on the cement floor. The case was cracked, but the laptop continued to work for one more day before it completely crashed in Buenos Aires.

Like many business travelers, I used to work during flights with my laptop placed on the beverage tray. I ceased doing this after seeing a large gentleman rapidly recline his seat, crushing the computer of the lady passenger sitting in the seat behind. The laptop became wedged between the back of the seat and the beverage tray, and the screen shattered and broke away from the computer.

These incidents demonstrate how computers are vulnerable to demolition during a flight or when clearing security and remind me to use the flight time to read, relax, listen to good music, or enjoy a movie. By doing so, you will arrive at your destination much more refreshed and ready for the busy week ahead. Most importantly, you will arrive with a functioning computer. My experience is that you can forget about any form of reimbursement from the airlines, other passengers, or airport checkpoint security guards for damaged laptops. Best to keep the computer safely stowed away in your briefcase or backpack, in your complete control near your feet. I suggest never stowing the laptop in the plane's overhead storage bin as it can fall to the floor when passengers open the overhead compartments to store or retrieve their items. If you use the storage bins, do not stow the computer out of sight, especially on long overnight flights.

There are times when we must work during a flight when finishing a presentation or preparing for the upcoming week. I have found that if you explain to the agent at check-in that you must work during the flight, they can block the seat next to you, providing you with more working space and a safety zone from others. Planning and advanced notice may work wonders.

En-Route Alcohol Consumption

Alcohol consumption on long overnight flights promotes jet lag, which potentially affects your performance several days into the trip.

The best policy is to minimize alcohol consumption en route. You want to arrive as refreshed and clear-minded as possible and not suffer from jet lag.

Customs Rules and Regulations

When arriving at all international airport immigration areas, one of the first signage you see is 'No Photos - Use of Mobile Phones Prohibited', or similar. I understand this regulation is focused on smugglers who can hide contraband inside the immigration area and then take a photo of the exact location for an accomplice who will later collect the smuggled items. I am sure there are other security reasons. The penalty for violating the laws can be substantial, such as losing your mobile phone and being arrested. Entering immigration in Uruguay, the businessman in line ahead of me took a photo of the area with his phone. Customs police immediately confiscated his phone, took him to a separate room, and threatened arrest. He later returned to the line, short his mobile phone, which I am sure was needed to execute his business trip. Immigration area photo and phone usage restrictions are the same worldwide but enforced differently. The safest policy is to keep your mobile phone and camera safely stowed.

In Equatorial Guinea, one of our colleagues was arrested for taking a photo of the president's residence. We all knew that photographing any government property in the country was strictly prohibited. The colleague lost his mobile phone, spent more than a week in jail and paid a hefty fine. An innocent act such as taking a tourist-type photo can jeopardize the business trip and be quite embarrassing for the travel team, especially if the client becomes aware of the incident, which was the case for this event.

Immigration Passport Entry Stamp on Arrival

Failure to receive an immigration entry stamp in your passport has the potential of seriously disrupting or terminating a business trip. When clearing immigration and before leaving customs, you should always be 100% certain that the immigration officer has clearly entered the visa entry stamp in your passport. If you do not witness your passport's stamping, ask the officer to point to the stamp.

Sometimes agents become distracted and do not stamp the passport, or the stamped seal is unclear. In some parts of the world, the failure to stamp the passport may be intentional and is a means to penalize you when you depart the country if the passport has not been legibly stamped. In that case, customs will note the omission when leaving the country and you may be detained until acceptable evidence is produced supporting your legal entry into the country. Alternatively, you may have to pay a hefty fine. This process can be extremely time-consuming, expensive and may prohibit your departure on the scheduled flight, affecting meetings for the remainder of the trip. Lastly, note the visa stamp's passport page location. You may need to point it out to the agent on departure, as stamps are often difficult to locate in a nearly full passport.

Interestingly, as I wrote this chapter while traveling on holiday, my hotel requested a copy of my passport visa entry stamp to waive a hotel tax, but I could not find the visa entry stamp in the passport. Before leaving the country, I spent a full day at the customs office resolving the issue that would have been avoided had I noticed at the airport that customs had not stamped the passport when I entered the country. Additionally, I paid another fee to process the new visa at a bank remotely located from the customs office. Fortunately, this was a personal trip and I did not lose a full business day managing the issue.

Several years ago, our travel team of three arrived in Uruguay, and our boss was sitting in the front of the plane and was the first person

to deboard. He raced out the plane door to immigration. There was no immigration agent present and he continued out of customs and waited at a bar for my colleague and me to clear customs. When we joined him at the bar, he bragged about how fast he flew through immigration and customs. Three days later, as we left the country, the customs agent could not find the entry stamp in his passport – because there was none. He was apprehended and taken into custody. My colleague and I could do nothing. We assumed that was the last time we would see him on the trip, so we boarded the plane to Miami for a meeting scheduled for the following day. Fortunately, Uruguayan customs released our colleague and the plane kindly waited 10 minutes for him at the gate.

The bottom line is always to ensure that the customs agent stamps your passport when entering any country. Never 'run' past an immigration checkpoint, even if no agent is present. Hopefully, these stories will serve as potent reminders of the importance of passport visa entry stamps.

Security Delays Resulting from Multiple Visas

In the early 2000s, I often traveled with a South African colleague who traveled extensively throughout Africa, the Middle East, the Far East, Russia and the ex-Soviet countries. His passport was extraordinarily thick from continually adding pages for new visas. After September 11, 2001, when international security was highly elevated, we made several trips together. Because of all the Middle Eastern visa stamps in his passport, when clearing US immigration and customs, it was a certainty that he would be pulled aside and his luggage would be thoroughly searched. He would then be escorted to a separate room and questioned. The process always took 30 minutes or more. We can now laugh about those experiences. I always jokingly told him that the problem was his full beard and worn suitcase, which looked like it had also traveled the world. He did have a moment of

supreme pleasure when he was waved through Brazilian security and I was taken off for questioning.

As a global traveler, the takeaway from this story is that specific country visa stamps in your passport can create unplanned immigration security delays. Therefore, extra time should be budgeted into the planning.

Passport Control

When changing international flights in certain parts of the world, immigration officers often ask for your passport, saying they will make a copy and be right back. Never lose sight or control of your passport. My experience in many parts of the world is that you will get it back after negotiating and paying a fee. Tactfully ask the officer not to leave with your passport, then ask another airport official for assistance. Alternatively, offer the officer the laminated passport copy that you carry. There is absolutely no reason for your passport to be taken out of your sight unless all passengers are required to relinquish their passports, in which case I still suggest never losing control of this document. Also, never let these agents see any significant amounts of currency you may be carrying.

Intra-Country Small Airline Flight Safety

You will work in developing countries at some point in your career and the only option for intra-country flights are often old, poorly maintained aircraft. I have taken flights in Africa, overloaded with passengers – one passenger sitting in the co-pilot seat and the cargo holds also overloaded with luggage and other freight. Flying between small airports in Mexico, both engines stalled at flying altitude over dense jungle. The engines were restarted, we landed, and I reported the incident to the local airline manager. I also wrote a detailed letter to the airline's customer service department and did not receive a

response. Flying on poorly maintained small aircraft is a risk we might assume as international business travelers. Do your best to evaluate the safety of small airlines in the trip planning stages.

Different Arrival and Departure Airports

You must closely review your itinerary for connecting flights that depart from a different airport, most common in large international airports when the connecting flight is a domestic flight, either on the same or another airline. For all connecting flights, ensure in the early planning stages that you are aware that the next leg of your flight departs from another airport. Also, ascertain that your luggage is checked to the final destination and prearrange ground transportation accordingly.

Travel Expense Control and Business Class

Many corporations have policies that allow business class travel for flights over a stated number of hours, for example, 9 hours. I had colleagues who always flew business class because they negotiated employment contracts permitting this. Others fly business class because of their seniority, and others for medical and physical reasons. Some international business professionals live on airplanes, so my comments below do not apply to these travel warriors who certainly deserve the extra comfort of business class.

Over the years, I have always banked travel mileage points that could have been used for business class upgrades. However, I prefer to accumulate the miles for leisure trips to visit countries I have developed a particular interest in through my business travels. Occasionally I receive business class upgrades because of airlines' frequent flyer programs, otherwise I fly economy class with upgraded extended legroom. Business-class fares are expensive and I want my company to know that I am prudent in managing business travel costs.

However, for an excruciatingly long trip requiring, for example, a total door-to-door travel time of 18 hours or more, a business class seat is a reasonable request, especially if you are a bit older and need the extra comfort.

I travel economy class for three reasons. Firstly, I became accustomed to economy seats during a severe business downturn. Everyone in my company (including the CEO) was required to fly economy class to reduce travel costs. After several years of traveling in economy class, I learned to tolerate economy seats. Secondly, I believe being frugal with travel costs minimizes opportunities for someone in accounting (or elsewhere in the company) to jeopardize my ability to travel as frequently as I consider necessary by making an issue of my travel costs being extraordinarily high. It can become a significant problem for an international traveler when someone in accounting, who is not familiar with the high cost of international travel, has a vendetta against your travel expense reports. I needed to maintain the freedom and the flexibility to travel as frequently as necessary to develop business opportunities. I had colleagues who experienced persistent criticism from the accounting department and others because of their excessively high travel costs, principally flying business class and expensive wines. This became an issue for the colleagues who earned a reputation for their large expense reports. As a result, all their travel planning and related costs were continuously under the microscope, and they did not feel free to travel as frequently as the position required.

I have been extremely fortunate to have had substantially complete control over my travel planning throughout my career, with limited oversight from others. This benefit, I believe, was because I earned the reputation of being a frugal business traveler, which is particularly important now as a consultant. Having said the above, the client must never perceive us as cheap. As I mention in Chapter 15, we should entertain the client at the restaurants they prefer. The

client interface is not the activity in which cost-cutting efforts should be directed.

In planning each trip, an excellent practice before traveling is to meet with those in your company responsible for reviewing, approving and processing your travel expense reports. Use this opportunity to share your upcoming itinerary with the accountants and those who review and approve your expenses, then discuss your planning effort to control your travel costs (for example, economy flights). Also, discuss with these parties the importance of entertaining specific clients at the more expensive restaurants used by the local business community. Also, explain the reasoning for staying at the more expensive business community recognized hotels as discussed in Chapter 15.

After returning from your trip and before submitting your expense report, meet with the same people and explain any unusual costs incurred, such as the $150 bottle of wine that the client suggested you select at dinner. Colleagues who review and approve your expense report may not be familiar with your position's requirements or the cost of doing business internationally. Open and transparent communications with those responsible for approving travel costs will facilitate the approval of your expense reports.

Flying business class may be necessary to some people's image. Our project required meeting with upper-level executives and managers at Sonatrach, the Algerian national petroleum company. Our company policy was to fly economy class to reduce costs during the economic downturn. I was unsuccessful in communicating directly with the client to arrange a high-level meeting, so I turned to my network for assistance. The father of a former colleague had maintained a long-term relationship with the president of Algeria, and I asked my friend and former colleague if he might discuss our requirements with his father. Within a couple of days, the meeting was scheduled. This is an important example of why you should

maintain contact with those you no longer have direct business relationships with. My friend also had high-level contacts in Algeria, so we asked if he might travel with us. He was interested, and I mentioned that our company policy was to travel in economy class. However, his father did not want any ranking Algerians to see his son flying in economy class, reflecting poorly on the family. All travel decisions, including flying or not flying in business class, must be evaluated from standpoints of cost, culture, image, and these days, possibly health.

I discuss networking in Chapter 2; however, the point above is important to the networking discussion. When requesting high-level support from your network you must consider the value of the request. You only have one shot when asking for such high-level help. For instance, in the above example, you cannot go back to this high-level person in your network and ask for assistance in arranging a second meeting with, for example, the Algerian Oil Minister or anyone else unless you have first returned something roughly equal in value. You may have only one chip in certain high-level network transactions and you need to spend it wisely. All requests from your business network have various value levels and you should not spend that value unless it is the highest and best opportunity. We must spend our network chips wisely and always repay our sources.

One more observation about flying business class and client judgments. These comments are precisely the opposite of the Algerian perception of my friend in the story above. I have several experiences where the clients I had scheduled meetings with were on my arriving flight. I find it quite embarrassing to be sitting in Row 2A drinking a glass of wine and the client boards and sees me in business class, and then they sit in economy. This situation would be incredibly embarrassing if you had recently requested a contract rate increase from the client. I much more prefer to use the flight cost savings on a steak dinner and a nice bottle of red wine with a client.

Auto Door Slamming

This comment may at first seem minuscule and unimportant. North Americans often drive large and heavy automobiles, and the doors are also heavily constructed. Sometimes the heavier doors require a bit of extra force to shut. Internationally, automobiles are often much lighter. The same amount of force that we might typically use at home to close a car door will be excessive and might damage the lightweight door. Unfortunately, I unintentionally slammed the car door of a CEO's car, who I was visiting in Mexico City. Before I could apologize, he drove away. The following morning, I apologized. His response was, "It is not a problem. I am getting a new car next week anyway!" His comment did not make me feel any better. Taxi drivers are also extremely sensitive to door slams as their cars are typically very lightly constructed and easy to damage. You should remember this rule to lightly and politely close car doors and your foreign hosts will be pleased about your consideration and courtesy.

In-Transit Courtesies Therapy

International travel can be uncomfortable, nerve-racking and leave you tense. You may be irritated by those passengers who are not seasoned travelers and tend to slow the boarding process down. My experience is that this is particularly the situation during the holiday season when the airports are full of people who are not frequent travelers, typically families with small children and older people. Because of travel inexperience, they delay the security lines and are slow boarding and deboarding the plane. They slowly stow their carry-on items, block the aisle and often sit in the wrong seat. This can be extremely irritating to the seasoned traveler who just completed a long week of meetings. One satisfying solution and therapy for coping is to look for these inexperienced travelers and then offer to assist them in any way possible. By doing this, your headache and tense feelings will go away. Try it next time. You will arrive much more

relaxed and ready for business. As Mark Twain said, "The best way to cheer yourself up is to try to cheer somebody else up."

In-Transit Restrooms

To close this chapter, my experience is never to pass up an opportunity to use an available restroom, especially in developing countries where public toilets may not be as common as you are used to seeing. Most international travelers have seen people squatting in airport corners and other public places while their companions use their coats to shield them from view. Try not to get into this embarrassing predicament. They say that a wise and campaigning politician never passes up an opportunity to use the restroom or eat a sandwich. Carry in your briefcase toilet tissue and emergency urination bags designed for travelers who find themselves needing relief and no toilets are available.

International travel is fun, exciting and often very challenging. I hope that the stories I have shared above will help you remember the points made.

CHAPTER 15

In-Country Logistics and
Hotel and Restaurant
Tools

COMPLEX INTERNATIONAL BUSINESS TRIPS can be exceedingly challenging because of all the moving parts and a tight schedule, all managed in a foreign environment. This chapter is designed to assist you in delegating specific organization responsibilities to local resources, allowing you to focus more on the business. It also alerts you to specific threats that have the potential of ruining an otherwise successful business trip.

Investment in Local Business Community Preferred Hotels and Restaurants

While fully understanding that this is the decade of frugality and being thrifty has become socially acceptable, premier hotels and restaurants are often vital to developing international client relationships, then later the client's project. Your selections must meet the client's expectations. Taking your client to a modest scale restaurant and staying in budget hotels may be perceived by others as cheap or as your company not sufficiently financially strong to take on the client's project. Being frugal may also raise concerns that your company 'nickel-and dimes' its operations and is not serious about the relationship. As well, taking the client to a ridiculously expensive restaurant might be perceived by some as an indicator of bribing. It would be best to research your client's expectations and the local business customs relative to the hotels and restaurants you use for client relationship development purposes.

In some countries, clients often prefer to meet outside their offices over breakfast, lunch, dinner, or drinks at the higher-profile business recognized and centrally located hotels and restaurants. These clients are typically frequent patrons and expect management and staff to greet them by surname. This is a form of respect and recognition of position in many countries. These clients will not accept invitations to lesser-quality venues. The main point is to project a positive image of your company to your client. You should never book hotels based solely on cost and reward points. The premier hotels will be more expensive; however, these costs are largely mitigated after thoroughly evaluating the logistical benefits of location, security, concierge support, business office support, and facilities for hosting client meetings. When referring to premier hotels, I mean business-oriented hotels and not a luxury hotel attached to a casino, found in many international cities and inappropriate for business.

Larger clients typically have a special corporate rate at the preferred hotels, which their executive assistant is usually happy to recommend and arrange. Selecting and booking the appropriate business-oriented hotel and restaurants will require some investigation, and as discussed below, the executive assistant is always the best information source. Never delegate hotel selection to your travel agent or others who cannot perform the required client research.

Lastly, remember that premier hotels provide an elevated security level for you and your client in countries with high-security risks. Working in these countries can often be tense and the premier hotels offer the international traveler a safe zone and much-needed peace of mind at the end of a long and stressful day. In some parts of the world, the hotel may feel like an oasis from urban chaos.

Client Executive Assistant Support

Seeking the assistance of the client's executive assistant is important. Company executives come and go, but the executive assistant stays, typically for decades or an entire career. This vital person is the absolute best resource for determining the client's restaurant preferences, meeting locations and times. After the meeting is confirmed, ask the client if you might communicate directly with their assistant for planning purposes. Bring a small gift for the executive assistant to express appreciation for their support.

Hotel Concierge

The hotel concierge service is another vital travel resource for trip planning and execution. Before travel, analyze the areas that professional concierge services can support your trip, then formally communicate your requirements to the hotel manager, requesting that he connect you to the head concierge. Always discretely tip the head

concierge upfront and handsomely, depending on your service expectations. Consider the following potential areas of concierge services:

1.   Arranging car service for arrival and departure flights.
2.   Restaurant choice, reservations and reconfirmation.
3.   Arranging and paying for hotel auto services.
4.   Reconfirming flight schedules.
5.   Special event tickets and services.
6.   Arranging gifts for the client and executive assistant (flowers or candies).
7.   Assist with check-in and checkout if you are short of time.
8.   Arrange for early check-in and late checkout.
9.   Assist in receiving client guests on arrival at the hotel, escort to the hotel restaurant, arrange transportation for guests and more.
10. Communicate and confirm meeting and restaurant destinations with drivers.
11. Reconfirm meetings, breakfast/lunch/dinner appointments with the client's executive assistant via phone call.
12. Manage the receipt and delivery of packages and documents.
13. Assist in arranging support from the hotel business support office, including having copies of documents made and outside printing support.
14. In general, provide an extra set of local eyes, ears and hands.

The head concierge's tenure at major international hotels is typically long-term, entirely analogous to the executive assistant's tenure previously discussed. These professionals will be there when you return on succeeding trips. The value of their support increases as projects develop and your hotel stays become more frequent and for more extended periods.

Other Hotel Considerations

International flights often arrive in the early morning. Booking an early arrival hotel reservation is important as most hotel check-in times start around 15:00. Arriving at the hotel at 07:30 and waiting hours to check-in is unproductive and physically exhausting, especially when you have been flying all night. Book the hotel for early arrival and reconfirm the reservation with the hotel manager or concierge.

If you are a frequent guest at a particular hotel, identify several rooms that meet your requirements and expectations, then request those specific room numbers when making the reservation. You will know exactly what to expect and will not be concerned about being in an unfamiliar room near an elevator, next to the ice machine, at the farthest end of a hallway, not on a safe floor, or the noisy street side of the building. Your room selections should be sufficiently close to emergency exits and on a floor that is high enough up to allow sufficient warning in the event of a terrorist attack or fire, yet not too high that an extended fireman's ladder cannot reach the floor.

After several trips and stays in the same room, you can ask the hotel manager to reserve 'my room', as my good friend does globally in all his favorite hotels. The added security and comfort provided by a premier hotel with a familiar room allows you to sleep well, focus on the business and not be preoccupied with hotel room issues. When checking in and before committing to a room you are not familiar with, always ask first to see the room and ensure no safety concerns or irritants discussed above. Do not be shy about asking for a room change for any reason. Consider the low profile or more recently constructed hotels engineered to withstand a major earthquake in earthquake-prone areas. Traveling to Mexico City soon after a devastating earthquake, the centrally located and older Hotel Camino Real met these requirements - a low-profile, stalwart, four-story, five-star hotel.

Lastly, my experience is that the more expensive international hotels are popular venues for weekend weddings, especially in Middle Eastern countries. Booking a room with a pool or garden view may be perfect during the workweek; however, weekend weddings are typically held in these areas and are often accompanied by loud music late into the night, making it impossible to sleep. It is important that you inquire about any scheduled weekend event activities when selecting rooms.

Restaurant 101

Internationally, many more popular restaurants are inside the premier hotels, simplifying planning and reservations. Restaurants inside upscale hotels are the most secure for cities with high-security risks.

Restaurant reservations should designate a seating section most conducive to a business conversation - away from doorways, restroom entrances and free of excessive waiter and guest traffic. Private dining rooms are ideal for high-level lunch or dinner meetings, are extremely popular and must be reserved well in advance. If possible, go to the restaurant in advance of the meal to meet the manager and the headwaiter, evaluate the dining arrangements and make any necessary adjustments in the table location and seating arrangements. Advance tipping the head waiter will, of course, best ensure the highest level of services.

Company executives often suggest meeting at a specific restaurant. There is a quaint restaurant in Houston with a small round table in a corner and near the bar, which is ideal for hosting a business lunch. I made a lunch reservation at the restaurant, and upon arrival with my client, I noticed that the special corner table was open and asked the restaurant owner if we could take the table. He said, "No, that is the

Tidewater table, and Mr. Taylor (the CEO) will be here in 10 minutes. Please select another table." The ironic thing is that Tidewater was our competitor. My client wondered why my company did not have the same clout and have a dedicated table. Seemingly trivial things do matter.

For the initial client lunch or dinner, arrive at the restaurant at least 15 minutes before the reservation time and review your table's location and seating arrangement. Planned seating should facilitate the discussions, so client and travel team seating locations are important. Make sure you are not seated near a competitor, which has happened to me and might spoil an otherwise productive dinner meeting.

The team lead, or the colleague who has the primary client relationship, should meet the guest at the restaurant entrance. Before the appointment, you should communicate to the client where you will meet on their arrival, clothing color and exchange mobile phone numbers. I had experienced several embarrassing situations where the client and I were seated in a crowded restaurant for a prolonged time before we located each other. This risk is high for first meetings with clients. Also, you should provide the client with the restaurant address because many have more than one location. Going to a different restaurant is a common risk, embarrassing and a waste of valuable time. I once scheduled a client breakfast meeting at the Airport Hilton Hotel in New Orleans, where I had stayed several weeks before. I did not make a reservation for the breakfast meeting, only to arrive and find that the hotel had been demolished. You should always make reservations for all client meal meetings, even breakfast. The restaurant may no longer physically exist.

Restaurant Meeting Etiquette

Travel team colleagues should refrain from eating the complimentary breadsticks or ordering drinks before the client's arrival. Unfortunately, I experienced a situation where a team member was the first to arrive and he ordered and ate an appetizer. When the client arrived, the colleague's plate and table area were soiled with breadcrumbs and the bone marrow appetizer he had eaten. It was a very embarrassing situation.

It is important to understand the cultural differences in the sequence of subject matter discussions during the first client lunch or dinner. For example, in Anglo-Saxton countries (Northern Europe and North America), the business is typically discussed at the front end of the meal. It is customary first to get to know each other in Latin countries and then later discuss the business.

For follow-up trips, a dinner the night before the official client meeting presents the unique opportunity to discuss, very briefly and in a more casual atmosphere, the important agenda items to be addressed in the formal meeting the following day. This approach avoids the client being surprised by the information that would otherwise only be presented for discussion in the formal meeting. It also provides an opportunity to resolve any issues before the formal meeting. Otherwise, try to use the meal as an opportunity to strengthen the relationship.

Before the meal, you should determine the clients' preferences (or non-preference) relative to alcohol. The travel team should completely conform to the client's preferences, which the client's executive assistant can provide. Travel team excessive drinking is never acceptable and can damage relationships, not only with the client but also with colleagues.

When meeting a client one-on-one for lunch or dinner, where to sit is frequently a question: shoulder to shoulder or across from each other. Each country has different business customs relative to seating positions, which should be researched before travel. Alternatively, stand and wait until the client suggests where you sit.

When you and a colleague are meeting a client for lunch (i.e., three people on a square table), do not sit the client in the middle as they will continuously be turning their head right then left to communicate with you and your colleague. Placing the client on one end makes it much easier to talk to both of you without turning their head 180 degrees, back and forth like watching a tennis match. In any seating arrangement, a pet peeve is when one person seems to turn and continuously talk to one person and excludes the third person. Some people do this habitually, and it is rude and irritating to the person excluded from the discussion who is continuously looking at the backside of the speaker's head. In any dialogue, when at the dinner table, move your head slowly between guests and speak to the total audience.

For the complex trip to South America referred to throughout the book, meeting with all the targeted clients within the time available required us to schedule lunches and dinners on weekends. Weekend time is the client's private time, and if not properly requested, the invitation may be viewed as imposing on their personal time and possibly rude. Understanding this, the invitation is more likely to be accepted if you explain the weekend meeting's reasoning and apologize for any inconvenience caused. Secondly, if you invite their spouse or partner to the meal, the client's likelihood of accepting a weekend invitation is enhanced. I have found that client spouses and partners appreciate being invited, and the client appreciates your consideration. Of course, weekend meal invitations are most appropriate for clients with whom you have a previously established relationship.

Intracity Logistics

Managing logistics for a complex meeting schedule in most large international cities is best accomplished by hiring a local car services agency to provide vehicles and drivers. The agency should be contacted early in the planning process to provide logistical information such as driving times between meeting locations and similar knowledge needed to develop the meeting schedule for the week. The hotel concierge usually is the best source for arranging transport services.

The travel team should travel together in a single vehicle. If the team is more than two people, the simplest transport option is a private car, a small van, or a Suburban hired through your hotel. Again, the concierge can arrange these vehicles. The cost can be charged to your hotel room, eliminating the need to carry substantial amounts of the local currency, negotiating the car service rate, or even worse, dealing with taxis. If your travel budget is limited, Uber or Lyft are excellent transport options now available in most large international cities. These companies offer modern and, if required, larger vehicles, such as a small van or suburban-type vehicle. Fares and services are charged directly to your credit card. Another transportation option is to call a local taxi service company, but the service is not always dependable.

Hailing a street taxi is the least secure and reliable option yet the most economical. When forced to use a street taxi, try to select a cab from which a well-dressed businessperson just exited. That taxi might be a safer option than a taxi that selects you from the street. It is extremely dangerous to get into a cab that has selected you. Before getting into the car, confirm that there is a meter and that it works. Alternatively, negotiate a fare in advance of getting into the car. To avoid language issues, I always carry a supply of pocket-size note cards and write the destination's address on the card for the driver, along with the agreed-upon fare. Alternatively, ask your hotel concierge to

write all the addresses for the day on the cards. The concierge can also verbally communicate the destination(s) to the driver if departing from the hotel. For longer taxi trips, request the driver to write the agreed fare on the notecard to eliminate end-of-trip rate negotiations. If the taxi driver does not immediately recognize the destination's general area, then take another cab. If your destination is in a remote or less secure part of the city, where taxis may not be readily available, then agree on the cost for the cab to wait. I have often been stranded in remote areas, unable to find a taxi. It would have been much safer to ask the driver to wait.

Always carry enough local currency in small bills. Taxi drivers never have change, and large bills are useless unless you do not expect to receive any change. If you are in a city where taxicab security is a concern, before entering the vehicle, photograph the license plate and the driver's taxi license, which is typically located on the back of the driver's seat, then text the photos to a party who is not with you. The diver must see you doing this.

Avoid Rental Cars

From my experience, I suggest not renting a car for several reasons. In large cities parking space is always limited and driving habits are usually significantly different from your home country. The risk of an accident is high, any accident will almost always be your fault and the delays will be incredible. Internationally, most vehicles are rented at and returned to the airport, typically located far from the city center. The time required to refuel, return the car, then negotiate the repair cost for any dents and scratches (which seem always to be found) reduces the time available for timely and more relaxed flight check-in.

Client Company Provided Vehicle and Driver

Your client may offer to provide transport using their company car and driver. This support is always appreciated and certainly avoids the issues associated with arranging third-party transportation services or a rental car. When using a client-supplied vehicle and driver, the travel team should never discuss any business matters while in the car. Unknown to you, the driver may speak English and completely understand, or potentially misunderstand, the conversations, which may be relayed to the client. Also, if the client meetings involve contract negotiations or other sensitive business discussions, there is always the possibility that your conversations are being recorded. Take the opportunity in the car to say positive things about the client or how much you appreciate the city and the country. If you must communicate delicate matters with colleagues while in a client-supplied vehicle, do so electronically by text message, email, or other digital communications. Alternatively, type your message on your phone and pass it to your colleagues.

Briefcase Security in Client Offices

When attending any meeting, never leave your briefcase or notes in the meeting room while you are out for lunch or leave the area for any other reason unless you securely lock it. Preferably it would be best to take the bag with you. During a meeting in another country and sitting next to one of the company's principals, I noticed that he was continuously straining to see my notes like someone does when trying to cheat on a test. Before we left for lunch, I was suspicious and placed the notes in my briefcase and set the zipper in a position that was easy to remember. When we returned from lunch, the zipper was in a different location. I am 100% certain that my briefcase had been opened and my notes copied. Having previously felt that the host appeared to be excessively interested in my notes, I wish I had written on the last page of notes: "I know you are going to copy my notes. I

hope you can read them because I have problems doing so!" I never again trusted this individual or his company, and I never returned, even though there was potential for future business. I always wanted to tell the individual, whom I know, that I was aware of what happened, but then I said to myself that "there might have been a mysterious force that caused that briefcase zipper to move on its own and how stupid I would have looked if that were true." My notes were not helpful to him; however, the briefcase's contents were needed for the trip and should have been taken with me and not left sitting unattended in the host's office.

CHAPTER 16

Health, Safety and Security

TO REALIZE THE GOALS of the business development campaign, you must maintain your health, travel safely and securely. Not placing a high priority on each of these areas has the potential of ending an otherwise successful trip.

Viruses

The international traveler is constantly exposed to viruses. Contracting colds and other viruses on long flights by breathing recirculated airplane cabin air have always been a travel health threat. The international traveler must take reasonable precautionary virus protection measures but not be paranoid or obsessed.

Travel Medicine Resources

The International Society of Travel Medicine is a reliable information source for travel-related health information and resources. Travel medicine departments of large hospitals also provide comprehensive pre-and post-travel medical care, including:

1. One-stop care, including all required and recommended immunizations, exams and preventative medicines for trips to any country.
2. Pretravel physical exams.
3. Phone numbers of US embassies and consulates.
4. Up-to-the-minute travel information.
5. Scheduled appointments.
6. Specialized follow-up care.

Travel medicine centers monitor global epidemics and pandemics, maintain vaccination records and administer required booster immunizations. These resources are vital to the international traveler's health.

Internal Security Risk Meter

A seasoned international traveler quickly develops a reasonably accurate instinct, or a gut feeling, for a city's security risk level. Amazingly, your internal risk meter is usually spot-on. Certain cities have reputations for being insecure, but you often find that they are not as bad as people proclaim after a short time in-country. Having said this, your gut may not be as dependable as the local crime statistics. When traveling to countries with high-security risks, it is advisable to enroll your presence with your country's local embassy or consulate, and this process can typically be completed online.

Before traveling, read country risk intelligence reports, which often discourage you from traveling or leaving your hotel without security support. Even though I read these reports, I always take the opportunity to interact with the local culture, such as walking through the local markets. In Algeria, not long after September 11, 2001, my company evaluated an energy-related project and the government provided an armed military escort for transport. The armed escorts returned our team to the hotel each evening and asked us not to venture outside the hotel premises. It was Ramadan and Algerian families were shopping for the night's iftar, enjoying the evening, walking between the fruit markets, pastry shops and very aromatic bakeries. The Algerians I passed on the street were extremely courteous and I felt safe and comfortable. This wonderful Ramadan evening walking among the people is what I remember the most about Algeria. Trust your intuition for security safety levels, but do not miss opportunities to mix with and better understand the local culture.

Airport Reception Security

Airport transportation agencies receive international business and leisure travelers on arrival. As soon as you clear customs, especially in developing countries, hundreds of people typically stand outside, holding signs with passenger names and loudly calling their names. You must ensure that the people receiving you at airports and holding signs bearing your name are legitimate. One control is using a code word or number that you establish with the transport agency. The primary risk is that third parties can obtain your name from other sources and prepare the sign with your name. Or they might steal the legitimate person's sign with your name with the intent to rob or kidnap you - or they only need the taxi fare income. This risk is global. In my hometown of Houston, well-dressed individuals approach passengers in the baggage area and offer rides into the city. It is extremely dangerous to accept their offers, regardless of how well dressed they are. To reiterate, never take any unsolicited assistance at

airports from people offering help with your luggage, transportation, hotels, money exchange, or anything else. For example, you might be arrested for exchanging money with individuals in or immediately outside the airport in Caracas. These arrests, or fines, are often schemes run by the local police.

Eating and Drinking on the Streets

We often travel to parts of the world where food and water are suspect. I have stayed in local hotels and drank from the water coolers in communal areas, only to later see the hotel staff refill the water cooler from the public water supply. I subsequently experienced a severe case of 'Montezuma's Revenge' in one of these hotels. Hotels in some parts of the world use non-potable water for showers. If this is the case, be careful not to drink any water while showering. Water sold in the streets in plastic bottles have often been refilled. Always check the bottle's seal. The best policy is avoiding water or food from street vendors and hawkers. Protein bars brought from home can be lifesavers if you are hungry and must immediately eat something. The energy bars are durably packaged and easy to pack in your suitcase and computer bag. Enjoy the trip and do not be overly concerned about food and drink. Just follow commonsense guidelines.

High Profile Escorts and Security

On trips to West Africa, companies often use armed escorts to transport their guests, executives and managers to and from the airport and for general transportation around the city. These escorts may carry large-caliber guns and the vehicles often have flashing red lights and use loud sirens. When traffic stops, I have seen escort personnel get out of their vehicles, walk forward to the car causing the traffic jam, then forcefully prod the driver with the butt of their gunstock. I have not worked in these countries for an extended period, so I do not fully understand the need for such high-profile and

forceful escorts. On a recent leisure trip to Egypt, our tour group was discretely accompanied by armed guards 24/7. Do not be surprised or alarmed by the extra security in countries you travel to, which may first appear to be excessive.

Kidnapping and Ransom Insurance Coverage

In my early years of international travel, annually I would receive a call from my company's accounting department asking which countries I planned to travel to during the following year. I assumed they were preparing the annual budget, and the purpose of the call was to estimate the travel costs. I later learned that the company was renewing the Kidnapping and Ransom (K&R) insurance policy on me. Companies that carry K&R insurance on their international travelers keep the coverage confidential, and they certainly do not discuss the dollar amount of coverage with their international travelers. This said, if you travel in areas recognized for kidnapping risks, it is advisable to ask your employer if you are insured.

Taxi Security

Most of my near-miss security incidents have been in street taxis. You are an easy target, especially as a passenger late at night on long cab rides between an international airport and the city center. You carry all your gear and possessions for the trip and taxi drivers and thieves know this. You have cash, credit cards, a laptop computer, a mobile phone, an iPad, a watch and possibly an expensive ring. The items are nicely packaged in your luggage, briefcase, or body-safe and easy for the thief to take. The monetary value of these items is significant to a thief in a developing country, or anywhere for that matter. The value goes up exponentially when considering the potential forced cash withdrawn from an ATM using your bank debit cards. Carrying all your gear in a taxi, you are highly immobile and an

inviting target for a thief. Your mobility is dependent on the size, location and the number of bags you carry.

Depending on your company's travel policy and your budget, you may be required to use local taxis. The typical theft scenario is when the taxi departs from the standard route to meet with coconspirators waiting in a secluded area. They take all your possessions and possibly you. Sometimes they take your shoes and clothes. I have had two taxi-related near-miss situations. I had to physically encourage the driver to stop the car and get out with my belongings for one incident. I walked to the main street, hailed another taxi, and arrived safely at the airport on time.

When riding in a taxi, always pay attention to the driver's demeanor and the route. Control over your luggage is enhanced by placing it inside the cab, immediately next to you – not in the trunk or boot. If the taxi's engine stalls, never follow the driver's request to get out and push the car to restart it. This may be planned, and the driver starts the engine and takes off with all your possessions. Always be aware of elongated routes to and from the airport, which is difficult to be mindful of at night for your first trips to the country. Mobile phone GPS is one security control for determining if the route is elongated. The best policy is to avoid street taxis and take a reputable car service from the hotel, for which you have prepaid the fare, charging to the hotel bill.

The following story is an example of improvising in a situation where your only transportation option is a street taxi. In the early 2000's we would fly to Caracas, Venezuela, arriving just before midnight at Marquita International Airport, located on the Caribbean coast, 19 kilometers from the center of Caracas. In those days, the airport taxis were a mishmash of old, large, beat-up and gas-guzzling US autos. The road to Caracas was (and still is) extremely dangerous at night, and taxis still have a reputation for robbing their clients en route to Caracas late at night. At the time, our US mobile phones

would not receive the local mobile signal at the airport or en route to Caracas. We could not communicate with our hotel or colleagues to confirm our arrival in Venezuela and provide our ETA at the hotel. One of my Dutch colleagues improvised an innovative security idea for managing this situation out of absolute necessity. In the presence of the cab driver using a mobile phone with no service signal, in a loud voice and speaking in English or our best Spanish, we would fake a call to the hotel as follows:

"Hello, this is Mark Lamb. I have a late arrival reservation at the Marriott. I am now boarding a taxi at Aeropuerto Maiquetia. Would you please write down the following information? My taxi is a blue 1982 Chevy Impala with license number VC1234 (then looking at the driver's taxi permit I.D.); the driver's name is Juan Romero, certificate number 1234. I will arrive at the hotel in 30 minutes. Thank you."

This is a brilliant and innovative security tool to use in a risky situation with no other communication or transportation options available. The possibility of the taxi driver robbing you has been virtually eliminated because, to the best of his knowledge, you have fully identified the driver to your hotel, along with a complete description of the taxi and an ETA at the hotel. We must think creatively to ensure security when traveling internationally.

One last point is that taxi security levels tend to follow the country's economy: a bad economy – high risk, and vice versa. When Buenos Aires was economically healthy and thriving, the taxis were extremely safe, with well-dressed drivers. As the economy went down, drivers needed money, and the once reliable and secure taxis became dangerous. Local economies dictate the taxi security trend wherever you travel.

Intestinal Issues

If you do not experience an occasional stomach issue while traveling internationally, you must not have dove deep enough into the culture. Most travelers will experience intestinal problems at some point, and travelers to the US or Europe are frequently sickened as simple changes in diet and water can affect anyone. Interestingly, the more you travel to a particular part of the world, the higher your resistance becomes. Try not to allow your fear of intestinal issues to prevent you from enjoying the international cuisine with your client. After traveling to Mexico for years and avoiding the famous street taco stands, I could not believe what I had been missing. Upon arriving in Mexico City, I now head straight to the same street taco stand near my hotel and enjoy my favorite, Tacos al Pastor.

There are solutions for intestinal infections. On a trip to India and Nepal, both famous for traveler's intestinal issues, my only stomach problem lasted a few hours after taking a drug that my doctor prescribed for the one-month trip. Solutions exist and minor precautions such as drinking bottled water are advisable and practical.

On a company-sponsored hunting trip to Mexico, entertaining a group of customers, one in our group always experienced serious stomach issues when in Mexico. On his last (and final) trip with our group, we crossed into Mexico in four-wheel vehicles, which allowed the gentlemen to transport 100% of his supply of food, water and drinks into Mexico. Absolutely nothing that he consumed during the trip came from Mexico. On the second day of the journey, he started experiencing the same symptoms and stomach issues as his previous trips. He was ill and complained for the hunting trip's remaining two days. He instantaneously felt perfectly well, precisely when we crossed back into Texas. His change in condition was exactly that of a seasick person who first sets foot on solid ground—instantaneous recovery.

After witnessing this, I am convinced that some people can mentally make themselves physically sick without consuming any food or water in the host country, as was the case with this fellow traveler. The paranoia of getting sick can make some people sick, and constantly feeling insecure can result in being robbed. These people should not be traveling to countries in which they are uncomfortable. If you harbor excessive fears of safety or traveler's illnesses, an international career is not your best professional choice.

Jet Lag

Jet lag might affect you on one trip and not another. It is like seasickness; I have seen lifelong sailors become seasick fishing in moderate seas. Jet lag affects people differently; however, being well-organized and relaxed on departure and sleeping well on the flight minimizes jet lag. Drinking alcohol enroute can also promote jet lag that can severely impact your performance during the first days of the trip. I have, embarrassingly, had jet lag cases that were so severe that my head fell to the table at an internal company meeting. You do not want to be in this condition when presenting or in a client meeting.

Flight Claustrophobia

Claustrophobia is undoubtedly not a 'health' issue, but I do not know where else in the book to discuss this personal phobia. Sitting in an economy section window seat on a long overnight flight and being blocked from the aisle by two large and sleeping passengers caused me to be severely claustrophobic. I simply cannot and will not sit in a blocked-in seat. I do not have any other phobias, and I have scuba-dived in caves and did not have such a severe feeling of claustrophobia. My travel agent is aware of the problem, and I continuously double-check my seat assignments before travel. If I find myself in a blocked-in seat, I do my best to change it. For me, this is a real fear of travel that I must control.

The point is that every traveler has fears and other issues that must be managed. In my case, for the plane seating issue, the solution is early planning and clear communications with my travel agent, the flight check-in agent and periodic reconfirmation of the seat assignment. Proper planning provides solutions for most travel fears, concerns and issues.

Traffic Safety

Always take extreme caution when crossing streets in countries where traffic flow patterns are on the opposite side of the street from your home country, such as in the UK for Americans. When crossing a street, the brain tells you to first look in the direction of traffic flow you are accustomed. In one step, having automatically looked in the wrong direction, a car, bus, motorbike, or bicycle can hit you. The travel team must watch out for each other when crossing streets and bike lanes. Also, the sidewalks in many cities are in poor condition, and we need to watch for holes and warn team members of these risks when walking. A broken ankle or fall-related injury will undoubtedly prevent you from finishing the trip.

Throw-Down Wallet

Another security and safekeeping technique for weekend free time touring in large international cities is carrying a separate throw-down wallet. You bring the day's cash requirement, an expired driver's license and a couple of other items to make the wallet look official. Should you get robbed, give the wallet to the thief. All your activated credit cards, current driver's licenses and other cash reserves are safely stowed at the hotel and the remainder of the trip is unaffected by the incident.

Personal Demeanor and Security

We need to project a positive demeanor when traveling internationally. If you are alone and look and feel insecure, you will attract and be an easy target for a thief. I have seen this happen several times. Our director, who traveled with us to Brazil, was terrified of being robbed in Rio de Janeiro. He was visibly uncomfortable, insecure and refused to go out for dinner after dark with our team. His demeanor was such that if someone came up behind him and yelled, "Boo!" he might throw his wallet into the air. One afternoon, he stepped outside the hotel to smoke a cigarette through a side door, and yes, a thief immediately robbed him in broad daylight. I often think about this incident and I am convinced that this person's demeanor was like a giant blinking sign to the thief that he was an easy target. The takeaway here is to look confident in your appearance, be relaxed and look around as you move about. Looking confident reduces the chances of being robbed. However, if you do get robbed, do not resist. Hand the thief a wad of cash or your throw-down wallet and hope that is satisfactory and he leaves.

Blood Clot Risk of Long Flights

After a long and stressful week of international business meetings, you are usually exhausted on the home flight. You settle into your seat, possibly have a glass of wine and then catch up on some of the lost sleep. Walk around the plane and exercise your legs during long flights to enhance the blood circulation in the legs.

I experienced a significant circulation issue when returning from Beijing, China. Instead of taking frequent walks up and down the aisles, I stayed in my seat and must have slept non-stop for most of the 16-hour flight to New York. I hardly moved. When I did get up, I could not walk. I had a sharp and constant pain in the calf muscle, which did not go away for weeks. You can be in good physical

condition and still experience a life-threatening blood clot on a long flight if you do not regularly stretch your legs and move around the plane. Set your phone alarm to get up and walk on long flights. This might save your life. For many of us, compression stockings effectively reduce feet swelling during long-distance flights with limited exercise capability.

Personal Hygiene on Flights and When Executing the Business Itinerary

We must be particularly aware of personal hygiene as we travel. We eat several meals on long flights, become dehydrated and enjoy a glass of wine or other drink. These activities contribute to halitosis, body odors and create the need to groom and freshen up periodically. I can think of nothing worse than sitting next to a passenger or interacting with a colleague or client who has piercingly bad breath and body odors. Equally important is to avoid wearing strong colognes or perfumes when flying or during business activities and interacting with clients and colleagues.

While flying, we often need to freshen up a bit using products that do not require much, if any, water. It would be best if you carried on board and in your briefcase a small toiletry bag for in-flight freshening up (toothbrush, mouthwash, toothpaste, deodorant, shaving materials and a comb). The Web is the best source for finding these products and suggesting unique ideas for maintaining personal hygiene while traveling.

Travel Diet

If you have ever tried to maintain a healthy diet while traveling for business or leisure, you know how difficult it can be. Airline food is not healthy. You can pre-order meals when booking your flight, or you can bring food onboard. When you entertain clients at lunch or

dinner, you will be going to the more popular restaurants and it may not be proper to order only a salad and tea while your guest and colleagues enjoy a nice steak and red wine – especially in Buenos Aires. Fortunately, when traveling abroad, you tend to walk more. If you work in an early morning exercise routine, you can do a respectable job burning the extra calories consumed. For me, one of the greatest joys of travel is the opportunity to enjoy local foods and wines with clients and colleagues. Life is a tradeoff and you can work the extra calories off as you go and when you return home. If your guests and colleagues are enjoying a beer, wine, or other alcoholic drink and you do not drink, then order a non-alcoholic beer, a virgin mojito or a club soda and lime in a cocktail glass – not a water glass. One option is to tell the bartender what you will be ordering, and then you will not need to explain it to the waiter. At client meals, cocktail receptions and the like, it is important that we blend into the atmosphere to the extent possible. Client-related events are not proper occasions to air your personal beliefs on alcohol consumption, smoking, religion, or politics. Blend in.

Security - Walking in Unsecure Areas

Should you find yourself walking in a dangerous part of a city, day or night, you need to keep moving confidently, in the direction of safety, be it towards a taxi, a well-lighted business, or towards any other area of safety. Walk along the edge of the street, or if there is a median, walk there. Do not walk along a poorly lighted sidewalk near buildings and alleyways at night. I found myself in a situation after a football game in Buenos Aires, where a gang of teenagers followed me closely, presumably because I had a camera and a small backpack – both of which I should have left at the hotel. The neighborhood was so dangerous that taxis did not go there (always a good sign of an insecure area). I moved to the center of the street and walked swiftly until I located a taxi several blocks away. The small gang followed closely behind me the entire distance. In a problematic situation,

walking near the street or on a median provides a certain protection level not available on the darker sidewalks.

Pickpockets and Luggage Security

Many large cities are well known for their professional pickpockets, such as Madrid and Rome. We tend to be more aware of this risk when in these cities. Pickpockets are universal and travelers attract thieves who depend on this informal wealth redistribution system. Take every precaution possible to protect your possessions on your person, in your briefcase and your backpack. Avoid carrying loosely hanging small purses or small day bags. You will lose items to a pickpocket at some point in your travels. They are professionals who approach you in ways you cannot imagine.

In Rome, a woman with a crying baby and several children came to me and pointed at the baby's mouth, indicating that the child was hungry, then she tried to hand the baby to me to occupy my hands. Before I knew it, two of her children went for all my pockets. Another pickpocket incident was on a freezing night during the New Year's Eve celebration in Madrid's crowded Plaza del Sol. I was wearing a long winter overcoat, and the pickpocket pulled a wallet-like packet from my hip pocket, entirely from under the long and fully buttoned coat. To his disappointment and my luck, the packet was full of teabags. Loss of wallets and passports from pickpockets and other theft is common in crowded areas. You must do everything possible to protect your wallet, passport and all the items you are carrying - all vital in realizing your trip's business goals.

Never let your luggage outside of your sight at the airport or at any other time. Thieves are waiting for that one second when you are not watching. My wife and I were traveling in South America and we left our luggage in the boot of the car. In broad daylight and at a seemingly safe place, I was responsible for watching the car while my wife and

her friend looked for hotel rooms. We parked at a petrol station and in front of the restroom, near the station's office door. I quickly went to use the toilet and in less than 2 minutes, all the bags were stolen from the locked car. It was amazing that it happened in that location and as fast as it did. The thieves were waiting patiently for the right moment to strike, and I gave them the few seconds they needed.

Try to use an airport porter service if you are traveling with more luggage than you can easily manage. Use a cable lock system to control several bags when you are waiting to check-in, having a meal, or using the restroom. As a traveler, thieves are watching your every move and you cannot ever be complacent about the luggage's safety. Never leave your luggage in a taxi when you must temporarily leave the car for any reason. Take the luggage with you. It is too easy for a cab driver to drive away with all your things. If a police officer stops him, the driver will say he assumed that you had taken all your belongings - one more good reason for not placing baggage in the boot of a taxi.

Health and Emergency Medivac Insurance

International business travelers should not travel without health and emergency medivac insurance, especially during pandemics. Traveling to Egypt during the COVID-19 pandemic, proof of medical coverage was required to enter the country. If your company provides health insurance, ascertain that you are covered when traveling internationally, including medivac coverage. Medical evacuation costs are staggering, potentially hundreds of thousands of dollars, depending on your medical condition, location and where you are transported. If your employer does not offer these coverages, negotiate a reimbursement to purchase trip insurance coverage readily available online from major travel insurance carriers.

Bed Bugs

At first, this subject may appear trivial and inappropriate for a business travel health discussion. I have learned the hard way that bedbugs can create health risks and negatively affect business and leisure trips. It is important to be aware of the bed bug threat and avoid infestation as you travel and potentially bringing the pest home. Bed bugs live in hotels globally—One Star to Five Stars. One of Donald Trump's luxury hotels reportedly did battle with this pest. First, the bug's bites are incredibly irritating. They will make it difficult to sleep, and if you bring the pest home, the cost of a professional exterminator to properly eliminate the insect can exceed $2,000, plus the cost of a new mattress. Sleeping while continually bitten by bed bugs is impossible – while traveling or at home.

To minimize the risk of bringing bed bugs home, never place your luggage on the top of hotel beds. When you return home, use a luggage stand and unpack your bags in a room separate and far from your bedroom. If you live in a warm climate, open all suitcases in the outside heat and let them sit open for a couple of days, preferably in direct sunlight. Place worn under clothing in sealable plastic bags and wash as soon as possible in hot water. Bed bug infestations will not terminate a business trip, but they can cause you to lose sleep. They will take considerable time and cost to eliminate once you return home.

CHAPTER 17

Control and
Maintenance of Nine
Critical Travel Tools

OUR COMMONSENSE ABILITIES ARE ordinarily sufficient to plan, control and protect the critical tools we rely on as we travel internationally. The recommendations in this chapter and throughout the book aid in backing up our common sense to protect these tools.

Nine Critical Tools

At least nine travel tools are critical to international business travel. These tools must be packed, transported and protected. If lost, stolen, or damaged, not having the use of one or more of these items

will negatively impact the travel plan, potentially jeopardizing the business goals of the trip:

1. Passport (also pack previously expired passport).
2. Visas (and visa entry stamps).
3. Immunization test results and records.
4. Credit cards.
5. Cash (US Dollars and foreign currency).
6. Mobile phone (including charging equipment).
7. Laptop computer (including charging cord).
8. Travel medicine documents.
9. Prescriptions and medical support devices.

Granted, the loss of a mobile phone or certain other listed items will not end a business trip, but not having the use of certain of these tools will challenge the most experienced international business traveler. On the other hand, losing a passport, visa, not having a visa entry stamp, or required travel medicine documents can potentially end a trip. Each tool's relative significance is different for each traveler and country on the itinerary. Your travel checklist must prioritize items to meet your personal needs, as I have done in the travel checklist included in Tool No. 7. Maintain direct control of critical travel tools by stowing them in your carry-on luggage. Never carry essential tools in checked baggage or stored in an overhead plane bin outside your direct sight and control. All are best kept next to your feet.

Passport

The passport is the entry key to all the countries on your itinerary. You cannot enter a country without a valid passport. For most countries, it must have no less than six months remaining until the expiration date. This time requirement may be different for each country on your itinerary. A US passport can be renewed at any time

before expiration; however, the US Department of State website suggests renewing it within nine months of the expiration date. Passport and visa renewal reminder alerts should be set up on your calendar. Your travel checklist is also a helpful reminder tool for recording passport renewal and expiration dates. Next to the passport item on your travel checklist, add: 'Expires on X date, renew by X date, X blank visa pages'. List visas on your travel checklist with corresponding expiration dates. Frequent international travelers must closely monitor passport and visa expiration dates to allow sufficient renewal processing time before the next international trip. It is highly recommended that you utilize a professional passport and visa service company for all passport and visa applications and renewals. This professional service cost is reasonable when considering the time requirements associated with managing the processes on your own.

Immigration agents will not stamp passport pages that are not specifically available for visas nor stamp over existing visa stamps. If visa page space is limited, new pages must be added by the issuer of the passport, the State Department in the US. Always expedite this process to minimize the time without your passport. Again, the best advice is to use a professional passport service company for all passport and visa matters.

You should always carry your passport, preferably on your person in a body-safe. Small bags and purses are vulnerable to loss, theft and pickpocketing. Also, carry your passport when traveling domestically. Situations may occur requiring immediate travel out of your home country, including personal emergencies or urgent business matters. Maintain current visas for countries where travel is highly probable. There may not be sufficient time to fly home, repack your bags and collect your passport. Business and personal emergencies occur, and not having your passport with you will delay a prompt and more direct departure. Should you lose your driver's license, the passport is used for identification to board domestic flights and is useful for other official identification purposes.

Photocopies of your passport should be maintained in multiple locations: in the cloud, in your mobile phone notes, on a USB flash drive, on your computer and carry a hard laminated copy. At a minimum, copies should include the ID page with the photo. Still, I recommend a complete passport copy for the digital copy. Carry several laminated copies of your passport ID page in your suitcase and computer bag. In a personal emergency scenario and not carrying your passport, I would hope that immigration would consider, in a dire situation, the passport copies ID page as a valid reproduction. I would not plan on immigration authorities accepting a passport copy, but you never know. You should also carry a copy of your birth certificate on your thumb drive, computer and phone. Combined, these document copies may be considered sufficient nationality identification to travel in an emergency should you not have a passport in your possession.

If you have an expired passport, pack it in your carry-on luggage. Should you lose your current passport, the expired passport should show that you are a citizen and carried an active passport before the current passport.

Security Documents

When entering government and corporate offices and facilities in many countries, you must present your passport for identification. Security agents often hold the passport to ensure that you return to the same security entry point and physically leave the premises. To keep physical control of your passport, ask the security officer if you could leave an alternate form of identification, such as a driver's license. For example, I have used expired driver's licenses at security checkpoints to maintain control of my passport in situations where I was concerned, for whatever reason, about the safekeeping and potential loss of the passport.

In many countries, when clearing corporate and governmental building security points and carrying a laptop computer, you may be asked to provide the laptop manufacturer's name and serial number, which will be verified when you depart the facility. Maintain this information on your mobile phone, speeding up the security check-in and checkout process. The serial numbers on most computers are extraordinarily long and in tiny numbers and letters that are difficult to read. Therefore, having this information readily available is extremely convenient. One other suggestion is to print the serial number using a tape label maker, then tape the number to the bottom of the laptop computer. I also suggest adding a tape label on the computer with your name, address, and contact data.

International hotels will always make a copy of your passport when checking in for identification purposes and as security for unpaid hotel charges and other outstanding costs, such as restaurant and car services associated with your stay. In the past and in certain parts of the world, hotels would hold your passport during your stay, but this requirement is now relaxed. In any case, if the hotel bill is not paid in full, the hotel will send a copy of your passport to the local police and airport immigration. You will not be allowed to depart the country until the hotel bill is paid. When checking out of the hotel, ask the clerk to confirm that there are no unpaid items. Car services and restaurant charges are often not promptly charged to your account. Remember to collect your passport if the hotel has held it as security.

Second Passport

US citizens can obtain a second passport, which may be issued based on specified circumstances. An internet search states that "A second passport is only issued if you are unable to complete your travel through a change of itinerary or you cannot cancel your current

passport to obtain a new one." There are other situations where a professional passport and visa service company can guide and help you apply and obtain a second passport. For example, traveling to Iran and Israel on back-to-back trips, I was advised to use separate passports for each country, separating the visa entry stamps. Again, obtaining a second passport is a matter to discuss and arrange with a professional passport and visa service company.

A second passport will have the same expiration date as the first passport. Therefore, the second passport can be used for travel while your first passport is in the process of receiving a visa for another trip or pages added. Of course, the second passport is superb insurance should the first passport be lost or is stolen. Remember, should you lose the first passport that carries a visa entry stamp, when departing the country, you will have to manage the issue I discuss in other chapters. If this happens, start addressing the missing visa stamp problem immediately to ensure that you depart the country as scheduled.

Financial Tools

Credit Cards

When traveling internationally, the worst-case scenario is the cancelation and loss of use of the card - not the risk of fraudulent charges, which you are not responsible for if you have promptly notified the credit card company. Credit cards are the most efficient and safest financial tool for paying hotel bills, restaurant checks, Uber rides, and purchases. Their use is safe because major credit card companies quickly adjust your account for fraudulent charges at no cost to you. The credit card company will cancel the card once you report the fraudulent charges.

Uber and Lyft transport typically only accept credit cards, and these services are now available in most large international cities.

Premium credit card companies will reimburse you for foreign transactions or ATM fees. The economics of credit card use are enhanced by requesting the payee to record the charge in the local currency to get the best foreign exchange rates on the card. However, many hotels and restaurants will use a fixed and less favorable US Dollar exchange rate, thus eliminating a credit card's foreign exchange rate advantage.

The international traveler should never rely on a single credit card. If your card is hacked, lost, or stolen, the credit card company will immediately cancel the card upon your request. If you have misplaced the card, for most major cards, you can place a temporary transaction hold through the card issuer's website; then reactivate the card when found. Always place a temporary hold on a missing card before canceling it. Otherwise, the canceled card must be physically replaced. Traveling internationally, it is often difficult to receive the replacement card on a timely basis, soon enough to avoid inconvenience and embarrassment when you do not have a card to pay for the client's lunch. If the card is canceled and you do not have a backup card, ensure that the issuing company clearly understands that you are traveling abroad and request that the replacement card be sent via overnight express mail. You should always carry a second and preferably a third card to use until you receive the primary replacement card. Backup cards should not be carried on your person. Consistently distribute your assets with this risk in mind.

Before leaving on your trip, notify all credit card companies of your destination and travel dates. I have had cards canceled after one foreign charge on the card because I did not communicate travel dates to the credit card company. Remember that automatic payments charged to the card are also canceled. To restore the auto payments, you must provide the payee with the new card information. It is convenient to maintain a listing of all autopayment company websites, passwords, and phone numbers on your password-protected travel thumb drive. This will facilitate the process and ensure that you do

not miss recurring payments while traveling. My experience is that trying to make autopayment changes by phone when on a business trip is time-consuming. Consider using a different credit card for autopayments and leave that card home eliminating the risk of loss or theft.

When using a credit card internationally, always maintain the credit card's physical control when paying a restaurant check. When you receive the bill, write the US Dollar equivalent amount of the charge on the credit card billing face. This is a control should the local currency amount charged on the card be grossly overstated by adding an extra digit, and you miss the accidental or intentional error. Waiters will typically bring a credit card reader to the table to process the transaction. My suggestion is to blot out the security code on the back of your card with a felt tip pen and keep the 3-digit code recorded separately in your mobile phone or elsewhere. If you do not control the card, the waiter can copy the front, use the security code and fraudulently make electronic charges to the card. I carry each card in an RFID blocking sleeve. Placing the empty sleeve on the table is a visual reminder to retrieve the card from the waiter. I have found myself talking to my guest, not paying attention and leaving the credit card in the restaurant's check folder. Always return the credit card to its assigned location in your wallet or stow it in another security tool.

Cash (Emergency Reserve)

Carry emergency cash reserves of $500 to $1,000, then divide the money and store it in separate locations (i.e., wallet, money belt/body-safe, a hotel safe and briefcase) to spread the risk if one of these cash reserves are lost or stolen. Larger bills will easily fit into a money belt. My wife and I further divide the US Dollars and the local currency equally on personal trips. The hotel room security box is typically a safe place to leave excess cash and other valuables: however, set a reminder on your phone to remove all items from the security box when checking out.

You should carry an adequate local currency supply, but not too much, as exchanging excess foreign currency will always result in an exchange rate loss when reconverting. When I wrote this chapter, I was in Colombia, where the largest bill issued from an ATM was 50,000 pesos, or about $15. Typically, very few taxis and few businesses will have change for a 50,000-peso bill, so it is important to carry a supply of smaller bills. It is also necessary to bring small bills or coins for public toilets. With larger bills, as with 50,000 pesos, you may be out of luck at a public toilet in many countries unless you want to pay, for example, 50,000 pesos, to use the toilet. My experience is that taxis never have change for any size bill.

Currency Exchange

The best exchange rates for the local currency usually are at an ATM using debit cards issued by major banks. Many premier debit card companies will reimburse your account for ATM fees charged and will not charge foreign exchange fees. Where available, use ATMs safely positioned inside the bank or inside another secure area. Furthermore, someone should accompany you to the ATM and be alert for suspicious people who may be watching you.

Other options for exchanging your home currency for the local currency are at less favorable exchange rates. My suggestion is not to exchange money at your home departure airport or inside the host country's immigration and customs area, where there is typically a single currency exchange booth. The best airport exchange rates are usually immediately outside of customs, where you can shop multiple exchanges for the best rates. Hotels will exchange smaller amounts of currencies for guests only, but the rates usually are not as reasonable as you will get at the airport exchanges. Always recalculate the local currency amount of money exchanged, then discretely count it in the exchange clerk's presence, so people standing behind you do not see

how much money you carry. Again, someone should accompany you and watch your back.

Before traveling, research the country's official exchange rate and expect less than the official rate. I always prepare a currency conversion chart that I refer to when making purchases. I also develop a rough and quick mental conversion rate factor: a simple multiple or divisor that I convert the local currency to a rough US Dollar estimate. For example, a multiple of 3 or divided by 3 is the approximate US Dollar value of the foreign currency. You can also use web-based exchange calculation apps, some of which do not require a Wi-Fi connection; however, assuming you are on the street, using the app will require that you expose your expensive mobile phone, possibly to a passing thief.

Currency Restrictions

I have traveled to countries where US Dollars were the only currency accepted for substantially all transactions, except for hotels, which would only accept a limited number of major credit cards. I also traveled to countries that accepted only US Dollars for all transactions, including hotels, as was the case years ago in Angola. To make transactions in certain of these countries more complicated, they accepted no torn bills or any with issue dates of more than, for example, five years. You must thoroughly research credit card and foreign currency requirements in the country you plan to visit. The more remote the country, the more complex the money management issues are. My wife and I traveled to Tanzania for a safari. The travel agency's instructions were that all safari-related payments were to be made in $100 bills, each in excellent condition, which we carried. What they did not tell us was that no bills could have issue dates older than five years. All the bills we took were in excellent condition, but most were too old. We had to have money wired to the safari guide company in Africa. Again, to emphasize, thoroughly research the local requirements for all transactions. Today, most countries accept and

want US Dollars, but the bills must still be relatively current issues and good conditions. A new $100 bill that was previously torn and now repaired with tape may be worthless in the country.

I suggest taking approximately 100 of $1 bills for tips and incidentals. It is surprising how useful these dollar bills are, and there is no need to worry about the $1 bill issuance dates.

Airport Departure Taxes

Always check with your travel agent to confirm that airport departure taxes are included in the ticket price. If not, you must have sufficient cash on departure to pay the tax before receiving your boarding pass. Years ago in Colombia, the departure tax was as high as $50 to $70 and you paid the tax in cash at the airport. Many non-Spanish-speaking travelers stood in a long check-in line for over an hour, then later learned that the airport departure tax is payable at a different location, with another long line. The current trend includes the airport departure tax in the ticket price. However, countries that need US Dollars or Euros may require the tax paid in US currency at the airport on departure. Therefore, it is important to be aware of the airport departure tax requirements and plan accordingly. It is amazing how many passengers do not have sufficient cash to pay departure taxes and struggle to find the cash minutes before their flight departs.

Online Money Transfer Platforms

My experience is that financial matters requiring immediate attention tend to wait until you travel abroad. Setting up a web-based fund transfer app, such as PayPal, before travel is an excellent tool for transferring money and making third-party payments while traveling outside your home country. Funds are quickly and safely transferred and payments made worldwide from your bank account or by credit card charge. Transfers or payments are typically completed within three or four days. For example, some platforms allow transfers up to $3,000 to select countries in multiple currencies for a reasonable fee.

Having these applications set up before travel will save time and cost when making these transactions while traveling internationally. Your comprehensive travel checklist should include activating a money transfer platform.

Other Cash Considerations

Carry only the currency needed for the day and keep it organized. You are creating an unsafe situation when your currency bills are disorganized and you are openly digging around in your wallet or purse trying to find the correct amount of currency to pay a taxi driver or vendor. A thief will see that you have a wad of cash, and you become a larger target than you already were before you started digging in your wallet or purse. For extreme emergency cash requirements, bring two or three blank personal checks, as in some parts of the world, you may be able to write a check for cash at a correspondent bank of your home bank.

Safe Keeping Tools

The primary requirement for a safekeeping tool for cash, credit cards and passports is that the device works, it is comfortable to wear and that you consistently use it. Reliable safekeeping options are available in the form of wallets, money belts, or body safes worn under your clothing. I have used all these tools and ultimately feel more comfortable with one device than the others, and I stick with it. Not only should the product be comfortable, but it must also be technically well-designed in a manner that reduces the unintentional loss of items stored inside – it must be entirely idiot-proof. For example, once I did not fully zip-close a body-safe attached to my belt and worn inside the pants and credit cards fell down the inter-pants leg.

Another vital consideration for body safes worn inside your pants, secure them at the belt's buckle end. When using the toilet, going

through airport security, or changing clothes, the safekeeping device can easily slide off the belt's non-buckle end, down your leg and out the pant leg and be lost. This has happened to me and I was fortunate to have recognized the situation before losing my money, passport and credit cards. When clearing any security point, I suggest placing all personal items in a small nylon stuff bag to control better the items removed (wallet, belt, watch, jewelry, body safekeeping devices, coins and other loose items). Control is lost if these items are placed in the open containers provided or if items are placed openly on the security machine belt.

Especially important, after removing any item from their assigned storage location, always consistently return the item removed to the exact designated carrying location. For example, after removing and using a credit card to check into a hotel, I thoughtlessly placed the card inside my passport – not back in the card's assigned location. Later, when paying a restaurant bill, I went to the regular credit card storage location and it was not there. I was unsure whether the hotel clerk had returned the card to me or if I had lost it. After hours of searching, I found the card inside my passport. If I had not found the card, I would have needlessly canceled it, losing the use of the card for the remainder of the trip. So, always return all critical items to their assigned carry and hold location. Consistently carrying, packing and storing these items in the same safe place will be one of the best habits you will develop as an international traveler.

After flying all night and arriving in Amsterdam, I was frantic that I could not locate a small wallet containing all my credit cards and some cash. I located the airport police office and asked if anyone had found and returned a wallet. If not, I wanted to file a loss report. The police officer asked me to sit in the waiting room. I sat down and waited for 15 minutes and noticed that I was the only person in the room, wondering why the officer had not called me forward. I suddenly remembered where I had hidden the wallet in my bag, which was in a location different from where the wallet was normally stowed

and safely carried. I told the officer that I had found the wallet. He laughed aloud, saying: "Most people who rush in here are certain that their money, credit cards, or valuable item were lost or stolen. After they sit down in the lobby and relax for a few minutes, they suddenly remember where they placed the missing item. We skip all the unnecessary paperwork and they go happily on their way. Enjoy your time in the Netherlands and have a good morning!" Avoid situations like this by being consistent in stowing items in their assigned safekeeping locations.

Many things happen simultaneously, both physically and in our minds when traveling. In addition, we are a self-contained moving unit, carrying all the tools necessary to execute the trip. As a result, we frequently are tired, anxious, rushed and often confused about where we have stored items, as in the story above. For these reasons, it is extremely important to emphasize that being highly organized adds to our relaxation and clear thinking as we travel.

Travel Team Expense Sharing

Cash, credit card management and expense reporting are simplified by agreeing with your travel team in advance of travel, who will be responsible for paying the various trip expenses, such as meals, taxis and other costs. This understanding requires each travel team member to assume specific financial responsibilities and bring the necessary resources and tools to pay the agreed-upon costs. For example, knowing in advance who will pay for the client dinner avoids confusion when the check is delivered to the table. It is best to decide who will pay the bill and then communicate this information in advance to the waiter. Often, one of the travel team members will have a special relationship with the client, and they may prefer to take the lead for the team and pay the check.

Planning travel team expense sharing organizes and simplifies the process. My experience is that some colleagues will not bring sufficient cash or the appropriate credit cards unless they clearly understand their responsibility to contribute. I once traveled with a colleague who carried one credit card, American Express. Only a few international restaurants and hotels in the countries we visited accepted American Express. On my first trip to Argentina, a colleague told me that Diners Club was a popular card to use in Buenos Aires, so that was my primary card for the trip. I very quickly learned that a limited number of businesses accepted Diners Club. Fortunately, I carried a backup card, but it was clear that I had not done enough trip planning research to determine the most widely accepted credit cards.

Mobile Phones

The mobile phone is an indispensable travel tool that must be protected to the greatest extent possible. Consider the following:

1. Maintain battery and backup power using a portable power source. Battery power drains more quickly when traveling internationally because your phone continuously seeks signals. In addition, power connections are often limited internationally. Conserve battery power through Low Power Mode settings.

2. Always use the phone in a secure area, never openly on a street where someone on a bike, in a car, or on foot can easily pull it from your hand.

3. Ascertain that the phone and holster will not fall from your belt when using restrooms or clearing customs. For travel, I suggest using a secure mobile phone holster with a strong loop for wearing on the belt's buckle side. I have lost phones because of poorly designed belt clip holsters. The belt loop holster also serves as a protective case when carrying the phone in your

briefcase or bag. Everyone has their preference. Just be sure it works properly.

4.   Fully understand your phone's settings for data, phone service, and text messaging. Unplanned use of international data, text and voice is costly in most areas of the world.

5.   Before travel, research various international travel plans your phone service provider offers, including 'as used' daily travel passes or similar. These plans are incredibly cost-effective and are especially useful to contractors who do not have a company-issued phone and plan.

6.   As mentioned before, always turn your phone completely off in client meetings.

A colleague and I walked to a meeting on a very crowded sidewalk at lunchtime in downtown Rio de Janeiro. We arrived at the client's office and sat at a conference table, waiting for the client. I heard a phone ring from my briefcase, pulled my phone from the bag and pushed the answer button, but no one was on the line. The ringing sound continued from my bag. I looked more closely at the bag, and there was a mobile phone clipped to my bag's shoulder strap. It certainly was not mine or my colleague's phone. I answered the call and the gentleman speaking said that I had his mobile phone. I provided the phone's owner with the client's office address and left the phone with the receptionist. What had happened, when walking on the busy sidewalk and passing near the phone's owner, my briefcase brushed his mobile phone, clipped to his belt, then his phone attached to my bag's shoulder strap. My colleague and I thought this was hilarious. The odds of the gentleman's phone attaching to my bag's shoulder strap had to be infinitesimal.

This story is a memorable example of how a valuable tool, such as the mobile phone, will find unbelievable ways to escape from you.

Critical tools are magnets that attract loss, destruction, and theft risks. Protect the phone with the highest level of security.

Computer Backup and Security

The laptop computer is your primary tool for report writing, email communications, PowerPoint presentations and much more. Losing computer data and files while traveling is often difficult to replace. You may rely on cloud storage in your home country, but WiFi access in the countries you visit may be limited. Back up your computer regularly with an external USB portable hard drive. Instead of leaving the laptop exposed in your hotel room, lock it in a suitcase (I use plastic wire ties to keep honest people out of my luggage). Most hotel security boxes will now accommodate a large laptop computer. I often alert the hotel manager that I have computers and other equipment in my room, and not all items will fit into the room's security box. This tends to shift greater responsibility to the hotel to ensure that the equipment is secure.

Prescriptions and Medical Devices

Many of us have prescriptions and medical devices necessary to support our health as we travel. Medical items must be carried on our person or in carry-on luggage and protected in the same manner as you protect the computer, cash, and passport. Should the trip be extended, pack enough prescription medicines for the travel period, plus an emergency supply. I suggest at least doubling the estimated quantity to be consumed. Today, many people use mail-order pharmacy services, which require a week or more to receive prescriptions. Routinely check your prescription inventory several weeks before travel and allow for sufficient shipping time and other potential delays. I maintain several weeks' supply of medicines in my pre-packed luggage. Consider carrying medications in two batches in separate locations. For those who take a variety of medications, small

zip-lock pill pouches take minimal packing space and are perfect for apportioning morning and evening prescriptions.

Also, consider asking your doctors to write prescriptions that can be filled internationally and copy these to your travel thumb drive. Having pre-written prescriptions will save time by not needing to consult a local doctor. Also, bringing an extra pair of eyeglasses is vital for many of us with a copy of the prescription on your travel thumb drive. It is important that you are thoroughly familiar with your medical insurance coverage and review and understand the coverage provisions and limitations. As previously discussed, if your company does not provide emergency medical evacuation coverage, consider purchasing private coverage readily available online at reasonable costs then request reimbursement from your company.

Carryon Clothing for Arrival Meetings

If your luggage is temporarily misdirected or delayed, you may be without proper business clothing for a day or two. Always wear and pack in your carry-on luggage sufficient clothing to start your meeting itinerary, including a jacket, tie, dress shirt and slacks. These items, combined with articles in your carry-on toiletries bag, will get you through the first day or two of meetings and dinners before your luggage arrives. I have seen too many colleagues attend two or three days of meetings in the same jeans and sweatshirts that they wore on the plane, and they felt extremely uncomfortable dressing so casually at client meetings and dinners.

Travel Thumb Drive Back-Up for Critical Documents

The international traveler should carry a thumb drive with copies of all documents and information needed for the trip, should the items be lost or stolen. I carry the following data on two micro-sized – durable steel constructed thumb drives, 24/7:

- Passport and Visas (preferably PDF all copy pages of the passport).
- Birth Certificate.
- Immunization records (including immunization QR codes).
- Health insurance cards.
- Driver's license.
- Bank and investment account information.
- Flight information and itinerary.
- Credit and debit cards (front and back).
- Credit card and bank auto payment information (payee website and passwords).
- Passwords for important websites.
- Eyeglasses prescription.
- Medical prescriptions.
- A PDF copy of your business card (used for printing additional cards when traveling)
- Resume (CV).
- Contact information.
- Generic corporate presentation, corporate brochure and other presentation information.
- Inventory of corporate slides.
- Elevator Pitch.
- Other items to support your trip.

Sensitive data on the travel thumb drive must be password protected, should it be lost or stolen. Some thumb drives come with built-in software that can store and protect the data on the drive using a password-protected 'vault', now available on high-quality travel flash drives. Otherwise, each file can be individually password protected by copying and pasting a PDF or photocopy of the document to a Word or Excel file, then password-protecting the file. Small keychain thumb drives made of durable steel are designed for rugged travel. I keep, 24/7, one drive on my auto keychain and another in my computer bag, maintaining the master files on my

computer, periodically updating the thumb drives. Lastly, the keychain thumb drive has a wide range of uses for anyone needing to backup important data that might be needed on the go.

Critical Tools and Hotel Room Service Considerations

I have stayed in hotels where the room attendants assigned to my room always took extra time to perfectly organize all my bathroom toiletries and personal items throughout the room. Sometimes, I would find personal items on closet shelves and drawers, and I might have forgotten the article if I had not looked for them when checking out. Sometimes I was unsure whether the extra organization was just exceptional room service that deserved an additional tip or if some items were so well placed that I would forget them. If this concerns you, ask the room attendants not to rearrange or move personal items from where you have placed them. This is always a judgment call. Another consideration is to tip the room attendants upfront, put a *do not clean* service card on the door, and ask the hotel manager that the room is cleaned when you are present. If you are concerned about others entering your room when you are out, place the do not disturb sign on the door and leave the TV on at a volume level easily heard from the hallway. When checking out, be sure to check all drawers, closet shelves and under the bed for personal items that you may have placed there or possibly rearranged by room service.

One final word, when packing critical items and all other items, never do so in a rush. I have failed to pack items needed for the trip when rushed. After receiving two separate express mail packages from my wife, I had all the prescriptions and other necessary items required for the trip that I failed to bring because I packed in such a rush. Take the time to pack each item methodically; otherwise, you will invariably forget tools which may impact the trip.

CHAPTER 18

Select Travel
Equipment, Tools, and
General International
Travel Advice

THIS CHAPTER HIGHLIGHTS SELECTED information from my travel journals not previously discussed that I believe may be helpful to international business and leisure travelers.

Luggage Preferences

I frequently traveled with younger colleagues from all parts of the world during my career. They tend to take immense pride in their ability to pack extremely light, and they rarely checked bags, even for the longer trips. My Dutch colleagues took pride in their ability to

pack for a week or more in a single small carry-on suitcase so they could arrive at the airport a bit later and go straight to the gate without checking luggage. This also speeds up the arrival process, not waiting for checked bags to arrive on the luggage belt. To them, speed and efficiency are paramount.

Without a doubt, not checking bags reduces the risk of in-transit loss and item theft. However, my experience is that checked baggage often arrives on the luggage belt before you clear immigration, canceling one benefit of not checking bags. Still, not checking bags eliminates the risk of theft and misdirected luggage. One other argument for packing light in a single carry-on suitcase is that most international taxis are tiny. The space available in the boot or inside the vehicle cabin is minimal. Two passengers with large luggage will not fit into a small cab, especially in countries where taxis run on compressed natural gas. There is no space for a large suitcase or bag with the fuel tank in the boot. So there certainly are significant tradeoffs for packing and checking larger bags or traveling light and carrying all luggage on board.

I cannot pack everything into a carry-on bag for a complex international trip. I overpack and my younger colleagues often tease me about my large suitcase and waiting for my luggage to arrive on the luggage belt. Still, I always have all the tools I need for the trip. I check my bags and carry on board a laptop computer backpack with all my critical items. I also box and check heavy and bulky items that are difficult to carry and move through airports, such as corporate brochures and other large meeting materials.

To control multiple bags and other items carried between any two points, I establish in my mind the total number of items I am transporting. If you have three items, which is a comfortable number to control, before moving, confirm that you have three items. This control works well when changing locations. When traveling, many things are happening at once and it is extremely easy to leave an item.

Things left in taxis, restrooms, trains, and airplanes are usually lost. Simple mental checks protect your gear while traveling.

Checked luggage occasionally is temporarily misdirected. As discussed earlier, carry all items essential to the trip on board, including sufficient business clothing, in case your luggage is temporarily lost. My experience is that misdirected luggage usually arrives at the hotel in a day or two; however, there are exceptions. Lost or misdirected luggage typically results from late check-in or in-transit flight changes, especially when the flights are with different airlines with tight connection schedules. The risk of misdirected luggage is compounded when the connecting airlines are in different terminals, or worse, different airports. You should always review the flight plan for these luggage connection risks, discuss these with your travel agent, then plan to check or not check your luggage, then pack accordingly.

All bags checked and carried on board should have two durable identification tags with your complete contact information, including your mobile phone number and email address. Also, maintain identification information inside the bags should the outside tags be disconnected. All suitcases and bags should have visible markings differentiating yours from similarly designed luggage. When collecting bags from the luggage belt, you must look closely at the identification tag to ensure it is yours.

Several years ago, I brought a new Orvis suitcase and checked it, priority handling, to Caracas. On arrival, I collected a brand-new Orvis suitcase with an orange and black frequent flyer priority handling tag. It was the first bag off the plane. I quickly grabbed the suitcase, cleared customs and was off to Caracas in a taxi. Halfway to Caracas, I received a phone call from a gentleman who said I had his brand-new Orvis bag with an orange priority handling tag. He said he had my brand-new Orvis bag with an orange priority tag. I would have sworn that I had the only new Ovis bag on that flight, if not all of Venezuela.

He said he had an extremely tight flight schedule for a connecting international flight and would be waiting for me on the sidewalk in front of the airport. My cab turned around and we rushed back to the airport. We barely had enough time to exchange suitcases before the gentlemen's flight departed.

I learned never to assume that your brand-new, expensive and unique suitcase is the only one on the plane. You must read the luggage tags before taking your baggage from the belt. This potentially trip jeopardizing travel mistake presents a perfect example of the importance of placing your mobile phone number (as well as an email address) on the luggage tag. I have noticed that airport security personnel rarely verify luggage tag numbers when passengers depart customs with their bags. This was once a very reliable - standard airport control to ensure that the luggage is yours. Always be 100% certain that you take the correct bag.

Before checking in, remove all prior flight luggage tags from your bags. When checking in, always double-check the destination tag and ascertain that your bag is going on the same flight and to the same destination airport, not a connecting airport.

Luggage Security

There is always the question of whether to lock checked luggage, secure the zippers with plastic electrical ties, or have the bag more securely wrapped and sealed in plastic. When traveling in certain parts of the world, you will notice travelers paying a vendor to have their bags wrapped in plastic. There is a reason for this. They probably live there and are aware of an elevated risk of baggage content theft, either in the local airport or at their destination. I suggest paying the local vendor to wrap your bags when you see this. I have found luggage locks useless as customs often cut the locks (even TSA designed). As noted above, an alternative to locks is plastic electrical

ties. At least you will know whether your bags have been opened or not.

One of my colleagues was a sheep farmer in a remote part of the Shetland Islands. He was also the contract manager for an operation in far northwest Russia near Sakhalin Island. It took him two days traveling each way and sometimes longer between his job and his sheep farm. His large and well-traveled suitcase was old and scared, in which he always carried several items of value. His security lock was a long, frayed, well-worn, one-inch diameter hemp rope. He said he never lost a thing from his suitcase in 10 years traveling across Asia and Europe, between home and work. He said, "People thought I was poor and they never bothered to open my suitcase." I thought his luggage locking system was a fantastic idea.

Luggage Options

Global travelers tend to become closely attached to their luggage and are incredibly particular about size, weight and general construction. International travel is extremely tough on luggage and frequent travel will require periodic luggage replacement. For this reason, I suggest purchasing luggage with lifetime warranties. The design must fit your travel requirements and be durable yet sufficiently lightweight to help meet airline weight limits strictly enforced globally. Well-designed luggage meeting the above criteria is expensive but is worth the investment.

Check luggage weights and weight limits before travel. Airlines strictly enforce baggage weight limits to control the airplane weight and the fees are an important source of revenue. A lightweight travel luggage scale is useful in packing at home and at the airport when reallocating items between bags to redistribute the weight to meet the airline limits. Without the portable scale, you will continuously have to reweigh the bags on the airline's scale. Also, be aware that luggage

weight limits can vary between the airlines on your itinerary. I have had situations where the departure airport allowed 50 pounds and subsequent flights on the same ticket had 40 pound limits. This is not an issue if the luggage is checked to the destination, but it is an issue if you collect your luggage en route, recheck it, and deal with the different airline weight limitations.

When traveling with others for business or pleasure, each traveler should always maintain complete control of their own bags - never switch bag control with others in your group. I have observed travelers inconsistently carry each other's luggage, ultimately leaving something behind. Carry and control your own luggage.

Bags Always Ready and On Standby

Frequent international travelers should keep their bags partially packed in an advanced state of readiness, 24/7. Pre-packing baseload items ensures that critical items are ready to go. Habitually reload all consumables in your travel bag after returning from a trip and unpacking at home, an opportune time to identify items packed that you do not need or use. Keep all consumables topped off and full, including prescriptions and toiletries. When it is time to travel again, the effort to finalize packing is minimal. This approach minimizes rushed last-minute packing mistakes and allows you to focus on other important trip preparation areas that cannot be completed in advance. As previously noted, it is imperative to pack at least twice the expected medication and prescription requirements as you never know if your trip will be extended. My anticipated three-week trip was extended to six weeks, and the supply would have been marginally sufficient if I had doubled the required medications. Lastly, if you have your shirts/blouses professionally cleaned, ask the cleaner to return them folded, not hung, and ready to travel.

For 16 years, I officed adjacent to our company's professional maritime salvage group, one of the oldest and most respected global marine salvage and emergency response companies for almost 200 years. These professionals are the best of the best in this profession. They stay in a constant state of readiness for maritime emergencies 24/7, such as ships and offshore drilling rigs sinking, on fire, vessel groundings and every type of maritime casualty imaginable. Each member of the salvage team maintains, in their offices, a fully packed, huge and heavy-duty duffel bag with the capacity to be at the scene of the incident for months. These incidents seem to always occur in remote and challenging parts of the world. Having worked with and around these professionals for many years, I learned how to keep a bag partially packed and ready for travel on extremely short notice. These professional responders always carry their passports, with current visas for multiple countries. They are 99% ready to travel on extremely short notice. They are splendid examples for the international business traveler.

Small Carry-on Toiletry Bag

I previously mentioned the importance of carrying a small bag of toiletry items such as a toothbrush and toothpaste, shaving oil, razor, deodorant and other items in your briefcase or computer bag. By freshening up a bit during a long flight, you will be much more comfortable during the flight and arrive more refreshed. This kit is also useful if your luggage is temporarily misdirected. It is always convenient to have these items readily available in my briefcase for occasional use during the business day, after meals and between meetings.

Duffel Bags

I have found that two (one small and one larger) lightweight nylon duffel bags are handy travel tools. They fold and pack neatly and

quickly. Duffel bags are useful for carrying items purchased on your trip and can be checked with luggage on the return flight. I cannot remember the number of times that I changed airlines with different weight limits and used a duffel bag to reallocate weight between bags to meet the airline's requirements. In many cases, it was worth the extra cost paid for checking the additional bag.

Microfiber Underwear

Men's and women's microfiber underwear are incredibly convenient for business and personal travel. I can very easily travel with only three or four pairs of underwear, all easily washed in the shower, quick-drying - minimizing the need to carry a large supply and having to depend on hotel laundry service's timely delivery.

Emergency Urine Bags and Toilet Tissue

I previously discussed the scarcity of restrooms in many parts of the world. There is an assortment of disposable urine bags on the market that are compact and easy to store in your computer bag or backpack. It is also advisable to pack a small supply of toilet tissue, often not available in any restroom, including at airports. Always carry a supply of local currency to pay for restroom usage. If you travel enough, you will undoubtedly find yourself at some point in dire need of a toilet.

Business Cards

Always pack an abundant supply of business cards. The primary use is for client meetings, but cards are also beneficial for any situation you need to leave your contact information (hotel concierge, restaurant maître D' and more). Many times, when communicating with people in the host country, your name may be difficult to spell

or pronounce. When presenting your name and contact information to another party, supplying your business card will simplify communications and reduce the possibility of errors due to language differences. You should always carry several business card supplies distributed in separate locations of your carry-on luggage to ensure an adequate supply. Maintaining a PDF copy of your business card on your travel thumb drive is useful if you need new cards professionally printed while traveling.

Prepaid Express Mail Envelopes

As suggested by my neighbor, packing a supply of pre-addressed and ready-to-send express mail envelopes simplifies mailing documents when working remotely.

Small Lightweight Day Pack

A lightweight nylon day pack is one of the items I see consistently recorded in my journals over the years. These day packs are stuffed into a tiny pouch, weighing almost zero and taking minimal space. A daypack is a must-have item and extremely useful for weekend excursions around the city.

Safekeeping Products

I had just returned to the hotel when I noticed that my wallet was missing. I soon received a call from the client saying that the driver found it in the company car's back seat. I was relieved, embarrassed and felt irresponsible. If it had happened in a taxi, I am confident I would have lost the wallet. The wallet had previously slipped out of my pocket on a flight; fortunately, I found it. After these two near-misses, it was time to find a workable solution to avoid losing credit cards and cash. The solution was a trifold wallet with a robust and

attractive chain attached to the belt. I have used these wallets for 18 years – 365 days a year, and I have never lost my wallet since.

Flashlights

At least two high-quality small micro-flashlights, with new batteries, are high-priority safety tools and are convenient to use as night lights when in unfamiliar hotels. Carry one in your backpack or laptop bag and keep one in your toiletry bag.

International Phone Plans

International phone plans are most important for contractors who do not have a company-owned phone and phone plan; however, these plans are excellent communication cost control tools for all international travelers. Subscribing to your service provider's global phone service plan will save money. Most carriers offer *as used* calling plans on a country-by-country basis. These plans provide a fixed daily charge for unlimited mobile phone and data usage for each country you enroll for the service. Voice calls, text and data costs are the same as when in your home country. The only added cost is the 24-hour country subscription cost. Enrollment is typically free and daily subscription costs may range between $5 to $10 for every 24-hour period in which the phone is used. Take the time to study these international service plans and determine which options are preferable for the countries you will be traveling in. If you plan to spend a significant amount of time in-country, consider purchasing an inexpensive local mobile phone, which will give you more of a local presence by having a local phone number.

CHAPTER 19

Conclusion

RECAPPING IN A FEW words, this book provides the international business development manager with experience-based guidance for the complete business cycle: network construction, business development campaign planning and execution, through participating in the tender process. All points presented are focused on respecting the client's time through well-organized and project-focused presentations – all based on a complete understanding of the client's project needs and providing project solutions. International travel skills to support trip execution are supported with take-away stories that will aid in remembering the points made.

My goal is that the information presented, and if consistently applied, will be key to your professional success. As stated in the Introduction, if I had this information when I began my career, my learning curve would have been much shorter and my confidence level boosted. Errors and mistakes made in planning and executing

international business development projects would have been minimized.

I want to highlight the importance of international experience to chief executive roles. International experience adds a dimension to top executive positions – principally understanding and assimilating into global working environments. Your accumulated international business development experience is essential to your advancement in today's highly globalized and technology-driven business world. The demand for business leaders who have worked internationally is stronger than ever.

The Toolbox section presents checklists, formats and other tools I have used throughout my career to plan and execute projects. These forms can be downloaded via my website listed below and should be modified to fit your needs.

Thank you for your time investment in reading the book. I am confident that the information I share, used as a compass and a map, will contribute to your success and provide guidance, vision and direction. I wish you the highest level of success as you navigate the turns and bends in your career path.

I would be pleased if you would share with me your individual experiences while applying my guidance. I also welcome any feedback on how you found the information and any suggested improvements. Send your comments, stories and thoughts to:
Mark33Lamb@Outlook.com.

I look forward to receiving your experiences and feedback.

Travel smartly, safely and often!

Part 5
The Toolbox

Toolbox Contents

Tool No. 1 – Pro-forma Trip Plan and Itinerary (Format)

Tool No. 2 – Checklist - International Business Trip Planning (Example)

Tool No. 3 – Client Meeting Request (Example)

Tool No. 4 – Agenda - Client In-Person Meeting (Format)

Tool No. 5 – Agenda – Virtual Client Meeting (Format)

Tool No. 6 – Checklist - Home Departure (Example)

Tool No. 7 – Checklist - Comprehensive Travel Packing (Example)

Tool No. 1 - Pro-forma Trip Plan and Itinerary (Format)

Notes and Comments – Pro-Formal Trip Planning
1. The trip planning document must be comprehensive and continually updated.
2. All confirmed items must be bolded to indicate that the item is complete.
3. As discussed in Chapter 4, the pro-forma trip plan will represent the optimum travel plan required to achieve the business goals. Every effort should be made to maintain the pro-forma plan. Ideally, the pro-forma trip plan and the final trip plan will be remarkably similar.
4. The pro-forma meeting plan must allow for sufficient time between meetings, provide for meeting time overruns and consider all the matters discussed throughout this book. When possible, limit the number of appointments each day and leave a day open at the end of the week to schedule meetings not planned initially, time to prepare meeting reports and minutes.

Draft Date:	
Revision No.:	
Destinations (in order of travel):	
Travel Period – From/To:	
Departure Date:	
Return Date:	

Changes made to this revision:
1.
2.
3.
4.
5.

Travel Team:
1.
2.
3.
4.

Targeted Companies and Primary Contacts:

Location:	Company Name / Key Contacts:	Priority (H, M, L)	Notes and Comments:

Summary of Meeting Days Available During Trip:

Country/City No. 1	0.0 days
Country/City No. 2	0.0 days
Country/City No. 3	0.0 days
Country/City No. 4	0.0 days
Country/City No. 5	0.0 days

Pro-forma Itinerary (All **Bolded** items are confirmed)

Trip Day No	Day	Date	Location	Schedule	Notes and Comments
				✓ 07:00 ✓ 09:00 ✓ 12:00 ✓ 14:00 ✓ 18:00	
2				✓	
3				✓	
4				✓	
5				✓	
6				✓	
7				✓	
8				✓	
9				✓	

Trip Day No	Day	Date	Location	Schedule	Notes and Comments
10				✓	
11				✓	
12				✓	
13				✓	
14				✓	
15				✓	

Notes and To Do:

Tool No. 2 - Checklist - International Business Trip Planning - (Example)

Notes – International Business Trip Planning Checklist
1. The trip manager should use this checklist as a guide for planning each international business development trip.
2. The checklist should be modified and expanded to meet each trip's requirements.
3. The checklist should become a living document and be modified over time.

No.	International Trip Planning Program Steps	Notes and Comments	Date Completed	Book Chapter Discussion
1	**Initiate Planning Process** - Begin the trip planning process well before planned travel dates, preferably 4 to 6 weeks in advance for complex – multi meeting international trips.			Chapter 6
2	**Preliminary Management Approval to Start Planning Process** – Obtain management approval to begin the planning process.			Chapter 5
3	**Travel Team Manager Designation** – Formally discuss travel team structure with management and designate Travel Team Manager			Chapter 5
4	**Travel Team Selection** – Select a well-balanced and knowledgeable travel team and obtain management approval for team composition. Communicate with the travel team the general travel plan.			Chapter 5
5	**Goals of the Trip** – Prepare the first draft of goals and objectives of the trip and review with the travel team			Chapter 4
6	**Goals Approval** – Prepare a formal copy of trip goals and submit it to management for comment and approval. Include			Chapter 4

No.	International Trip Planning Program Steps	Notes and Comments	Date Completed	Book Chapter Discussion
	approved goals in the travel planning documents.			
7	*Targeted Client Meetings* – Prepare a listing of targeted client meetings for each location in the itinerary. Determine the optimum order of travel locations (cities/countries) that best supports realizing the established and approved trip business goals. For each location to be visited, list client meetings in a logical order to accomplish business goals and objectives. (Note: This order of travel and client meeting sequence should be the best possible plan, unbiased by third parties at this point.) Do not over-schedule meetings and schedule sufficient travel days to accomplish the itinerary			Chapter 7
8	*Pro-forma Itinerary and Trip Plan* – initiate preparation of working document – Pro-forma Itinerary and Trip Plan - reflecting the preferred order of travel and client meeting order determined in the previous step.			Chapter 7
9	*Travel Team Review and Approval of Pro-forma Itinerary and Trip Plan* – Travel team to make comments and suggestions for changing the first draft of pro-forma itinerary and trip plan			Chapter 5
10	*Management Approval of Pro-forma Itinerary and Trip Plan* – Review the pro-forma plan with management and ask for their formal approval			Chapter 5
11	*Travel Budget Preparation and Approval* – Prepare a travel budget using the best available information. Obtain management			Chapter 5

No.	International Trip Planning Program Steps	Notes and Comments	Date Completed	Book Chapter Discussion
	approval for the travel budget.			
12	*Flight Plan and Availability* – Coordinate the travel plan with a professional travel agent and determine the availability of flights required to realize the pro-forma itinerary.			Chapter 6
13	*Provisional Booking of Flights* – Assuming that flights are currently available to realize the pro-forma itinerary, book travel team flights on a temporary - refundable and changeable basis.			Chapter 6
14	*Visas* – Arrange for professional passport and visa service to process visas for the travel team			Chapter 6
15	*Provisional Booking of Hotel Reservations* – Professional travel agent to confirm hotels that have been selected based on criteria outlined in Chapter 15.			Chapter 6
16	*Client Meeting Requests* – Make initial communications with clients, requesting meeting dates and times based on the optimum sequence of meetings presented in the proforma itinerary.			Chapter 8
17	*Pro- forma Itinerary Updates* – Maintain pro-forma itinerary and travel plan current by writing down dates client meeting requests are sent, and dates meetings are confirmed. All confirmed appointments, reservations and other information on the pro-forma itinerary should be **bolded** to indicate confirmation and finalization—update the travel team daily on the status of the developing pro-forma itinerary.			Chapter 7

No.	International Trip Planning Program Steps	Notes and Comments	Date Completed	Book Chapter Discussion
18	*Client Meeting Agenda* – Prepare a first draft of the meeting agenda to be reviewed and approved by the client (See Tools No. 4 and 5 and Chapter 8). Use the meeting agenda to communicate specific equipment requirements and other necessary planning.			Chapter 8
19	*Management Updates on Planning Progress* – Maintain regular and periodic communication with management about the status of the trip planning process. Avoid surprises relative to the planning process.			Chapter 5
20	*Client Updates* – Maintain frequent contact with the client, reconfirming the trip's status and other important information.			Chapter 8
21	*Logistics Planning* – Working with a travel agent, hotel concierge and client executive assistant – identify the company that can provide transport and logistics within the city.			Chapter 7
22	*Hotel Concierge Support* – Contact the hotel manager and discuss needs for concierge support during your stay at the hotel. Request hotel manager to connect you to the concierge and begin direct communications with lead concierge support			Chapter 15

Tool No. 3 - Client Meeting Request - (Example)

The following is a hypothetical example of email communication for making the initial request to the client for a meeting:

February 1, 2022

Dear Sr. Hernandez,

We will be in Buenos Aires the week of March 14, 2022. We would appreciate the opportunity to meet with you and your team to discuss our capabilities for supporting your water disposal operations at Vaca Muerta. If you are available to meet that week, could we first propose a meeting in your Buenos Aires offices on Wednesday, March 16, at 13:00 hours? We will keep our discussion to one hour or less. We are also available at 10:00 hours on Thursday, March 17. Please suggest alternate meeting days and times if these do not work for you and we will do our best to reorganize our schedule to meet yours.

Assuming you are available to meet, we will prepare and send you a short agenda for your review and approval, listing items we would like to discuss. Attached for your consideration are our corporate brochure and other information on our company.

Sr. Hernandez, thank you very much in advance for your time in November.

Best regards,

Mike Jones

Vice President of Operations
Shale Production Solutions
www.ShaleProductionSolutions.com
Attachment – Corporate Brochure

Tool No. 4 - Agenda - Client In-Person Meeting (Format)

Notes for Client In-Person Meeting Agenda
1. The agenda below is a general format for preparing an in-person meeting with the client and should be modified as required.
2. The first draft of the agenda should be sent to the client soon after the client has confirmed the meeting.
3. The client should be asked to modify the agenda as required.
4. The final agenda should be sent to the client well before the meeting.
5. All attendees should be provided with a copy of the agenda before the meeting.
6. The document should become a living document and be modified as required over time.

Area	Details	Notes and Comments
Agenda Draft Date:		
Client Company Name:		
Proposed Meeting Date and Time:		
Client – Primary Contact Name and Contact Data:		
Meeting Location – Physical Location and Meeting Room		
Client contact and contact date for meeting support items (i.e., meeting room location, projector, etc.)		
Attending – Client (Names and Positions)	1. 2. 3. 4.	
Attending - Supplier (Names and Positions)	1. 2. 3. 4.	
Meeting Objectives:		
Time Allocated for Meeting:		
Meeting Start Time: Meeting End Time:		
Client contact name for meeting room requirements:		
Proposed Agenda and Estimated Time (xx minutes):		

Area	Details	Notes and Comments
1. Introductions (x minutes)		
2. Discussion – Purpose of Meeting (x minutes)		
3. Review of Agenda (x minutes)		
4. Client Presentation (x minutes)		
5. Supplier Presentation (x minutes)		
6. Supplier Capabilities for Client Needs (x minutes)		
7. Open Discussion and Action Items (x minutes)		
8. Closing		

Client Provided Equipment for Meeting:
     1.   Projector
     2.   Extension cord
     3.   Electrical adaptors
     4.   Sound speakers
     5.   Stands for presentation charts and exhibits
     6.   Microphone
     7. Other		

Client suggestions and comments relative to contractor /supplier information to be discussed presented:		
Supplier questions and comments relative to information to be discussed and presented.		
Miscellaneous Notes and Comments:		

252

Tool No. 5 - Agenda - Virtual Client Meeting (Format)

Notes Regarding Virtual Meeting Agenda

1. The first virtual meeting will typically be of short duration and attended by a limited number of people.
2. When attendees are in multiple time zones, it is helpful for the agenda to list the different time zones should there be any time zone confusion.
3. Platform meeting information (platform web link, password, etc.) can be copied from the electronic invitations sent to attendees. This is a duplication of information sent to attendees and best ensures that they receive the meeting call-in information.
4. Attendee information should first list the client, then your company attendees.
5. The agenda should be as concise as possible and indicate who will be responsible for opening each item.
6. An agenda is an effective tool, even for a short meeting with a limited number of items to be discussed. The agenda provides structure and organization and will save time by maintaining organization during a video conference call in which multiple people attend.
7. The agenda should be sent to attendees as soon as the meeting is scheduled, requesting attendees to comment or amend the document. The final agenda should be resent to attendees before the meeting as a reminder and used in the meeting.
8. The document should be a living document and modified over time to meet your needs.

Client Company Name
Virtual Meeting Agenda
Meeting Date
(Approx. Meeting Time)
Attendee Location Times: #1 – 00:00
Attendee Location #2 – 00:00; Attendee Location #3– 00:00

Virtual Platform Call-In Information:

(Copy and paste here virtual meeting information, including meeting number and password)

Attending:

Client Company Name

Name #1
Position
Email address
Other

Name #2
Position
Email address
Other

Contractor/Supplier Company Name

Name #1
Position
Email address
Other

Name #2
Position
Email address
Other

Flexible Meeting Agenda:

1. Introduction of (Client Company Name) attendees (person responsible)
2. Introduction of (Contractor/Supplier Company Name) attendees (person responsible)
3. Client presentation (person responsible)
4. Brief presentation of (Contractor/Supplier Company Name) operations (person responsible)
5. Other discussion items (person responsible)
6. Action Items
7. Closing

Tool No. 6 - Checklist - Home Departure (Example)

<table>
<tr><td>

Notes – Home Departure Checklist

1. *This is a guide for preparing your personal checklist.*
2. *Activate this checklist one or two days before leaving.*
3. *Your personal checklist should be laminated and attached to the door that you exit from. To connect to the door handle, punch a hole in the upper left-hand corner and hang on the door handle with a string or rubber band.*
4. *Like all other checklists and form formats, the documents should be living documents that are continually modified to meet your needs.*

</td></tr>
</table>

1.   One Day Before Departure:

o   Business Phone – change voice message to out of office message
o   Cash - pack
o   Credit cards - pack and call company regarding travel plans
o   Airport holiday parking or Uber/Lyft – make reservations
o   Insect treatments – purchase and apply on departure
o   Mail – collect mail from the mailbox
o   Mail – complete postal mail stop forms and place in the mailbox or deliver to Post Office
o   Passports – pack
o   Plants – water plants and protect from weather
o   Packing – complete two days before departure
o   Travel itinerary and contact numbers – leave with a neighbor and family members, as required

2.   Immediately Before Departure – When Leaving Home:

o   A/C – Heater Wi-Fi – make sure thermostat is online – adjust temperature according to climate
o   Alarm system – turn on
o   All lights - off except hall/stairway light
o   Auto keys – leave home if flying
o   Ceiling fans and bathroom vent fans - turn off
o   Computers, printers and devices off and unplugged
o   Cookstove – make sure burners are off and gas valves are tightly closed
o   Dryer and washer - unplug
o   Front door – lock

o   Front porch light – turn on
o   Garage door – close
o   Garbage– take out
o   Heat and air conditioner – adjust up or down
o   House key to a neighbor (double-check neighbor's mobile phone number and email address)
o   Ice Machine – empty and turned off
o   Refrigerator doors – ascertain completely closed
o   Security cameras – turn on
o   Toilet bowls (3) – chlorine-based cleansers
o   Video camera – plugged in and online
o   Water - turn off the master valve
o   Water heater – off
o   Wi-Fi controlled lights – test and turn off or on as required
o   Windows (all) – make sure closed
o   Windows (downstairs) – lock
o   Windows closed and locked
o   _____
o   _____
o   _____

Tool No. 7 - Checklist - Comprehensive Travel Packing - Business and Personal (Example)

> ### Notes Regarding Comprehensive Packing Checklist
>
> 1. *This is my comprehensive personal checklist, from which I select specific items for each business or personal trip. You should develop a comprehensive checklist and continuously update it as required. Print the checklist and highlight the items you need for the current business or pleasure trip.*
> 2. *Begin packing at least three days before departing with the plan of being 100% prepared the day before departure.*
> 3. *Setting the suitcase on a luggage stand during packing and unpacking facilitates both processes.*
> 4. *This list can be laminated and attached to your luggage while packing, then maintained in your luggage – update as required. To connect to luggage, punch a hole in the upper left-hand corner and hang it on the luggage handle with a string or rubber band. Using a dry erase pen, you can check items needed, items packed and add items not on the list. (Certain items are intentionally duplicated in different sections of the checklist.)*
> 5. *Since the list is my list, it would be modified for a woman's requirements.*

This checklist is intended to be an all-inclusive, running list for business and personal travel. Scan the list and check items you intend to pack for your trip. Continuously update your checklist.

Documents, Cash and Related: 9 **Critical Items** – **To Be Carried On Board** – **not checked with luggage):**	Briefcase or Computer Backpack:	Miscellaneous:
o Current Passport – *(Memorize - Number 12345), Date Issued – _____, Expires: _____)* *Available Visa Pages – Sufficient)* o Previously expired passport o Home Departure Checklist - completed o Visas (list visas and expiration dates) o o	o Computer and accessories o Power adaptors o Several writing pens – ample supply (no gel pens which will leak at high altitudes) o International power adapters o Presentation and backup o External hard drive – ample storage o Business cards o Brochures o Notebook and pens o Client gifts o Reading glasses	o Luggage weight scale (lightweight) o Duffel bags for excess luggage (lightweight nylon) o Neck travel pillows (inflatable) o Woolite liquid wash soap o Moist towelettes o Leatherman tool (check with luggage) o Emergency urination bag o Luggage security cable o Books – limit number due to weight o Stain remover

o Credit cards (minimum of 2 cards)	o Hard case for glasses on flight	o 5" x7" envelopes for receipts.
o Cash – amount $_____	o Eye mask	o Supply of gator clips and paperclips
o Mobile phone and charger	o Face mask	o Small backpack/daypack
o Backup power bank	o Out of office notice	o European adaptors
o Laptop computer and charger	o Micro flashlight	o Plastic wire ties to lock luggage
o Prescriptions and medical support devices	o Breath freshener or mints	o Ziplock bags
o Business clothing (one-day backup)	o Fingernail trimmer/cutter – large (can be used for cutting other items and is typically allowed in carryon)	o Small roll of Gorilla tape (1 ft.)
o Electrical adapters		o Iodine solution to disinfect vegetables and fruits
o External travel drive (durable)	o Double-check seat pocket for items left	o Camera, memory cards and charging equipment
o Update key chain thumb drives	o Laser pointer for technical portions presentations (only if needed)	o Small gifts
o Passport copies (online/hard copies/thumb drive)	o Breath mints, sugarless gum	o Scented votive candles
o Airline ticket copies (online and hard copies)	**Reading, Entertainment, Electronics:**	o Electrical extension cords (2) (with adapter)
o Expired passport – take as a backup if others lost	o Books	o Hand cleaner
o Personal blank checks (3)	o Electronic book	o Compass
o Credit card copies (copies on a thumb drive)	o iPad (and charging cables)	o Ziplock bags
o Trip itinerary	o Computer and accessories	o Maps
o Health insurance cards	o iPhone	o Family photos
o Notecards and pens	o Backup battery	o Security whistle
o Credit card and bank websites and phone numbers, account numbers, email addresses	o Camera	o Travel journal
	o Camera memory	o Charcoal water purifier or water purifying tablets
	o Camera charging	
	o Backup computer before departing	
o Internet passwords – password protected	o iPad	o 1-liter collapsible water bottle
	o Charging cables	
	o Kindle and charging cables	**Auto Travel:**
o Hotel business card – address and contact information for your hotel that should be kept on your person	o Reading glasses and case	o Extra set of keys
	o Travel watch	o Road maps and atlas
	o Small portable "smart speaker" (for extended trips) and presentations	o Oil change
		o Tires rotated
		o Fluids checked
	Travel Memory Stick-Key Chain Thumb Drive (password protected):	o Insurance – Proof of Insurance
	o Negative COVID 19 test	o Travel pillows and blankets
		o Large cooler
		o Small cooler
		o Clear food bags (road trips only)
		o Cup of Soup

- o Packing full cubes for suits, shirts, pants
- o Packing half and quarter cubes for underwear, socks, ties and smaller items
- o Wheeled luggage

Business Trip Clothing:
- o Weather forecast for cities on the itinerary:
  - o
  - o
- o Travel jacket (blazer – wear on the flight)
- o Microfiber undershirts (dark color)
- o Microfiber underwear (dark color)
- o Dress shirts
- o Socks – dress and casual
- o Windbreaker/rain resistant coat
- o Sweater (light grey is excellent!)
- o Cufflinks (leave set in travel bag)
- o Reversible belt
- o Dress shirts (check for missing or cracked buttons)
- o Dress shoes and socks
- o Jacket – casual travel
- o Ties
- o Belts – casual and dress
- o Suit
- o Handkerchiefs
- o Tight leather shoes may not fit after flying all night

Leisure Trip Clothing:
- o Coat – lightweight down (rollup)
- o Kaki jacket
- o Jeans

- o Passport
- o Visas
- o Birth certificate
- o Internet passwords
- o Immunization records
- o Prescription copies
- o Eye exam prescription
- o Emergency phone numbers
- o Credit card copies (front and back)
- o Drivers' license copy

Sport and Exercise:
- o Bathing suit
- o T-Shirts
- o Walking shoes
- o Exercise shoes
- o Exercise socks
- o Exercise shirt
- o Exercise shorts
- o Exercise bag (radio, earphones)
- o Walking weights
- o Rain gear
- o Thongs or sandals
- o Rain suits
- o Sunscreen
- o Casual shorts
- o Insect repellent
- o Gortex rain gear

Security Items:
- o Money belt
- o Safety wallet
- o Body safe
- o "Throw-down" wallet
- o Computer model and serial number taped to laptop
- o Hotel fire mask

Personal Items - Miscellaneous:
- o Eyeglasses – backup glasses
- o Computer glasses
- o Sunglasses
- o Watch
- o Backpack/daypack
- o Reading glasses

Food and Cooking Items (Vacation Travel):
- o Travel food item checklist (prepare separately for each trip)
- o Electric cooking appliance
- o Stevia
- o Coolers
- o Cooking utensils
- o Smoothie powders
- o Breakfast drink
- o Oatmeal
- o Instant coffee
- o Fruit drink mix

Other:
- o Travel packing checklist
- o Toiletry-kit checklist
- o 100% "checklist "reloaded" toiletry kit
- o Clothing packing folders and bags ready to fill
- o Passport, visa, cash and credit cards
- o Body-safe(s)
- o Trip and meeting itinerary and checklist
- o Other items

Travel Snacks:
- o Energy bars
- o Turkey jerky
- o Dried fruits (sealed in plastic)
- o Cheese and Crackers – packed in plastic
- o Can opener
- o Plastic knife, fork and spoon
- o Gum and mints
- o Chocolate

Other Items for Current Trip (list):
- o
- o
- o

- Bathing suit (may double as workout shorts)
- Sandals or thongs
- Casual pants
- Shorts
- Polo shirts
- Cap
- Casual shoes (2 pr.) (walking)
- Rainsuit

<u>Toiletry-Kit – (Packed in Checked Luggage):</u>

- Toothpaste (with mouthwash)
- Dental floss
- Tylenol (Extra Strength)
- Deodorant pads
- Hair comb/brush
- Razor and blades
- Shaving cream
- Medical prescriptions (also in carryon)
- Vitamins
- Hair-care items
- Multi-use soap
- Laxative
- Benadryl
- Digestive medications
- Cold and flu medicines
- Digestive medications/pain relief medications
- Eye drops
- Sleeping aid
- Mini-zip locks for pills
- Insect repellent
- Wrist for motion sickness
- Allergy medication
- Other personal drugs and first aid items

<u>Toiletries: Carry On (and in a briefcase):</u>

- Prescriptions in small zip-lock pill bags
- Compression socks
- Toothbrush and toothpaste
- Deodorant pads
- Mouthwash
- Razor and oil shave lotion
- Medical prescriptions
- Medical devices
- Toothbrush
- Toothpaste (with mouthwash)
- Hard glasses case
- Sleeping mask
- Tylenol or equivalent
- Deodorant
- Hair comb/brush
- Razor
- Shaving oil
- Hard case for eyeglasses protection
- Earplugs
- Rinse free travel body wash
- Other things as needed per traveler
-

Note: Carry-on toiletry kit (small and light). should be carried in a briefcase on flights and during the day before and after meetings. Do not carry any sharp objects or liquids over 6 oz in the toiletry bag. Check these items. Double-check airline restrictions for carry-on items.

-
-
-
-
-
-
-
-
-
-
-
-
-
-
-
-
-
-
-
-
-
-
-
-
-
-
-
-
-
-

Suggested Further Reading

- ✓ *Range: Why Generalist Triumph in a Specialized World* (David Epstein. 2019).
- ✓ *"Work Hard, Study...and Keep Out of Politics!" Adventures and Lessons from an Unexpected Public Life,* (James Baker, 2006).
- ✓ *The Politics of Diplomacy – Revolution, War & Peace, 1989 - 1992* (James Baker,1995).
- ✓ *Speed of Trust* (Stephen Covey, 2006).
- ✓ *The Culture Map – Breaking Through the Invisible Boundaries of Global Business* by Erwin Meyer (Meyer, 2014).*Prisoners of Geography – Ten Maps that Explain Everything About the World,* by Tim Marshall (Marshall, 2015).
- ✓ *Kiss, Bow, or Shake Hands* by Terri Morrison and Wayne A. Conway(2nd ed. 2015).
- ✓ *Culture Shock – A Guide to Customs and Etiquette* (Series – multiple authors, published by Graphic Arts Center Publishing Company).

About the Author

Mark Lamb (CPA – Retired) graduated with honors from Texas Tech University with a BBA degree, majoring in accounting, and was recruited by Ernst and Young - Houston, where he practiced as a Certified Public Accountant for seven years, with a base of clients in the oil, gas, energy and maritime transportation industries.

For the past 35 years, his work has focused on international business development projects with global and domestic companies in the maritime industry. He has held board membership and executive positions with maritime industry associations, including the American Waterway Operators Association and the Texas Waterway Operators Association. He represented the US inland maritime industry at federal and state levels during the enactment of the Oil Pollution Act of 1990. He also worked closely with environmental interest groups to develop solutions for various maritime operation challenges in the US Gulf Intracoastal Waterway. He is a member of the World Affairs Council, Rice Baker Institute, The Hemingway Society, Asia Society – Texas, and attended the Rice University - Baker Institute Masters of Global Affairs Program in 2015. In semi-retirement, Mark provides business development consulting services

to international maritime operators, working from his home base in Houston, Texas. Mark can be reached at:

Email: Mark33Lamb@outlook.com

Website: www.marklambconsulting.com

www.ingramcontent.com/pod-product-compliance
Lightning Source LLC
Chambersburg PA
CBHW071548210326
41597CB00019B/3165